Endless Bloom

Planting Emotional Intelligence for Positive Growth

BILL MARKLEIN

Bloom BIG
God Bless,
WM

Published by Employ Humanity LLC.
Employ Humanity®

Printed in the United States of America.

Marklein, Bill, 1984–

Endless Bloom: Planting emotional intelligence for positive growth / by Bill Marklein

ISBN 978-0-578-68491-8

1.Emotional Intelligence 2. Leadership 3. Business

Thank you to my wife Stacy
for your endless love on this journey.
Thank you to my wife, family,
friends, clients, and community
who have encouraged and inspired me
to write this book.
At the end of the day,
we are all just walking each other home.

Contents

Take a picture of your book—
Share the ♥ on social media.

Introduction

In 2010, I earned my Master's Degree from the University of Wisconsin-Whitewater in corporate communication with a specialized focus on Emotional Intelligence (EI). I placed my energy into learning and growing within this field of study that has gained continued momentum since 2010. Teaching EI and seeing the positive impact EI development has on lives personally and professionally brings me joy and fulfillment.

At the time of graduate school, I did not fully know the magnitude that EI would play in my own success in business and life. The ability to effectively manage our own emotions and the emotions of others is essential for leadership as well as quality of life. I have yet to meet a great leader that does not have high EI or a relentless desire to improve it.

My passion is EI because it is what makes us human on our walk. Along my journey, I have shifted my focus to becoming the best version of myself. To successfully do this, I need to continuously look inward to process and learn from all emotions. The most positive exponential growth in my life has been during adversity, failures, and setbacks. To lead, serve, and inspire ourselves and others, we need to fully embrace both positive and negative emotions—and our humanity.

In 2015, I spoke at a conference in San Diego on the topic of EI. This conference, combined with another similar speaking engagement in Savannah the following year, was my awakening to how professionals in all positions and industries crave to learn more about EI. And with good reason.

EI is the #1 competency for success in and outside the workplace in roles that require leadership, teamwork, communication, and building healthy, trusting relationships. Additionally, EI is the source to optimizing human potential.

The story awaiting you will give you practical tools, character traits, leadership insight, self-reflections, group discussions, and inspiration that will plant Emotional Intelligence within you and your team for positive growth. The chapters are designed to easily visit and revisit specific areas of interest on your journey. I hope you enjoy this book as much as I did writing it.

Wishing you an endless bloom,

Bill

Chapter 1
Summer Pain

The university was quiet as most universities are on summer August days before the start of the school year. Professor Brooks Lambeau, dean of the College of Arts & Sciences, always appreciated these days as he stood in his third-floor office looking out the window on to the well-groomed landscape. Brooks moved to this top-tier university 25 years ago with his wife and two small children. The university had built state-of-the-art facilities, with the philosophy that you have to build the best to attract the best and deliver excellence.

This university was all that Brooks had in this chapter in his life. A tragic car accident had taken his wife two months after moving for the job decades ago, and both grown children now lived far away in different states. After contentious teenager years being a single parent, there had been no response in years from the outreach he made to his children.

The stillness of these August days always recalibrated Brooks for the opportunity to teach and inspire a new wave of minds, hearts, and souls. Brooks didn't have hard data but he did know within his heart that he had positively influenced thousands of lives throughout his life teaching. For Brooks, this brought much fulfillment of a life well lived.

Brooks was an icon at this university because he was a convener, imaginative, and passionate about the mission of the university to serve the region and world. Students enrolled here solely because of Professor Brooks Lambeau's glowing reputation to creatively teach and inspire. The university placed Brooks on task forces to recruit the best and brightest administrators and to help solve regional and global challenges. He certainly helped position the university as a driver for economic prosperity in the region.

Turning from the window, Brooks felt a sharp pain in his lower back. An avid cyclist and runner, Brooks was in excellent physical shape for his age. "Did I tweak it gardening this weekend?" Brooks questioned. He turned off his office lights next to a poster reading *COMMON SENSE IS A FLOWER THAT DOES NOT EASILY GROW IN EVERYONE'S GARDEN* and walked past the landscape he was minutes ago admiring from above and headed home.

The next morning the pain was present and more intense. Brooks decided to go to the university hospital where a body exam and tests would be performed.

His cell phone rang a week later. "Brooks, you will need to come to the hospital this week. We have found cancer and it is spreading," said his doctor.

Professor Brooks Lambeau, 61-years-old, was given six months to live.

Chapter 2
A Secret

The death-sentence diagnosis was sudden and came just two weeks before the start of first semester in early September. Brooks had fear, anger, and sorrow running through every cell of his body. He decided to walk campus at sunset and ponder how he was going to tell his children, administration, colleagues, and his beloved students. He found his favorite bench under a tree—the one with the best view of the student union fountain.

Brooks worked hard at mindful living. He did his best to observe life in the moment and found that this gave him a rich quality of life. Brooks made a habit of keeping a very small personal notepad in his pocket to scribe ideas, gratitude, and inspiration. Writing things down gave Brooks the ability to put thoughts into future action while also allowing him to immediately continue again in the present.

Memories flooded the mind of Brooks. Pure nostalgia. Memories of a life that's been loved. His 8th birthday party as a little boy with a new bicycle. His winning high school state championship touchdown catch. Meeting his wife for the first time. His children being born. Splashing his young children in the pool. The joy of teaching surrounded by brilliant minds. Fellowship with students, colleagues, and community members. "At the end of the day, we are all in the business of teaching and serving," Brooks thought. "The greatest gift and legacy is serving others."

Brooks also reflected on his most painful mistakes on his journey. "It's a wonderful life," Brooks thought. "I could have missed the pain, but then I'd have to miss the bloom. What a beautiful bloom."

These moments of pause, monitoring and processing emotions, always gave Brooks clarity. Sitting on the bench, a calm caressed Brooks. He had an inspiring idea and it involved keeping his terminal illness a secret.

Chapter 3
Creative Teaching

The energy of students returned to the university with new enthusiasm to learn, connect, and grow. Professor Brooks Lambeau welcomed students to his class "Emotional Intelligence for 21st Century Leadership," facilitated introductions, and announced an exciting new class format that he had designed. On the whiteboard largely written was *EI: BOLDLY HUMAN LIVING*. The class design, the playbook, was entirely built on Emotional Intelligence to prepare students for success in life. "My class, as it always strives to do, will challenge your thinking and inspire your mind, heart, and soul. This class will be unique, it will be creative," said Brooks joyfully. "Also, I know when you're texting in class. No one just looks down at their crotch and smiles." The class erupted in laughter.

His students' texting in class and constant interaction with mobile devices both frustrated and worried Brooks. He observed that students who were on their mobile devices most were significantly less creative and suffered more from anxiety and depression. "Who cares if someone doesn't respond to your text or social media post within an hour," he told his class. "Hopefully they are lost in a good book, hiking a bluff, or giving people they are with their undivided attention." High technology users were becoming increasingly robotic in their thinking and communications. "Digital obesity" is what one psychology professor at the university coined the digital addiction.

Students loved how Brooks connected nature and experiences to his teaching and mentoring. Brooks believed that Mother Earth was not only an abundant resource but also a teacher to successful living. Brooks did not admire people who lacked respect for Mother Earth and people less fortunate. Occasionally, students referred to Brooks as "Buddha" and "Yoda" on campus. Everybody knew who they meant when they did.

Brooks picked up a stack of papers and passed them out. On the bottom of each paper read *WHAT IS IT YOU PLAN TO DO WITH YOUR ONE WILD AND MAGICAL BLOOM?* Brooks continued speaking, "This is the class outline for the semester. You will see each one of your names on a morning during September and October outside of our regular scheduled class time. You will need to each meet me individually at the university coffeehouse at 7 a.m. on the day you are assigned. Make sure you arrive promptly and bring a notebook and your best writing utensil. Go enjoy the beautiful weather today and catch up with your friends you haven't seen all summer. Class is dismissed."

Chapter 4
Planting Emotional Intelligence

Minimalism and living within his means was the way Brooks chose to live his life. He took great pride in not owing anybody money and always preferred experiences more than things. Every morning Brooks would rise at 5:00 a.m., start brewing his coffee, and read his daily devotional which gave his day inspiration, clarity, and purpose. He would move on to the daily newspaper and always tried to read different angles to political and social issues. Different views positioned Brooks for improved empathy, an open mind, and more civil discourse.

As Brooks sat at his kitchen table, he reflected on his life. The best parts of his life were decorated with experiences. "Life is about experiences, not things," he wrote in his notepad. Over the years, he observed that the people around him who were continuously buying things to feel important or to impress others were empty inside.

There was an eagerness inside Brooks to start meeting with his students for the one-on-one scheduled coffee meetings. Big picture, Brooks wanted to plant the fundamentals that he was confident would position his students for success in life far beyond graduation. His principles were rock solid for success in and outside the workplace. Brooks observed the positive growth from these principles for young professionals all the way up to the C-suite. These principles were so effective for the C-suite that Brooks performed increasingly more executive coaching and consulting. Without question, Brooks found that the high-performing executives were lifelong learners and highly responsive to his coaching. "Even after winning multiple NBA Championships, Michael Jordan wanted to still be coached and challenged to grow," Brooks once said during a conference keynote. "The great competitors on and off the court are always trying to improve their personal best."

Speaking at conferences brought Brooks much joy and kept him energized and connected to fresh, diverse thinking. Brooks was an ambassador for building strong relationships and innovative partnerships with the private sector. He had excellent business acumen. He believed it was foolish and out of touch to stay solely in the silo of academia. "Theory is just theory unless it can be implemented in the marketplace," he would say to colleagues. Professors who stayed insulated were not effective in preparing students for current employer and regional needs.

Building a bridge to the private sector was a priority for the success of his university and students. This often led to Brooks making guest lectures in the MBA program and for chambers of commerce. Business summits and workforce development conferences were also the perfect stages to speak, and Brooks had full support from his university. "I do not consider myself a motivational speaker," Brooks was once quoted in a national business magazine. "I am a teacher of essential human-only skills. Motivation lasts a day, skills last a lifetime."

Brooks observed in his expansive years of teaching, coaching, and mentoring executives, athletes, colleagues, and students that an individual's Emotional Intelligence was the key predictor of success in life. "Remembering facts and figures is important, but how we connect with ourselves and others is imperative for success and optimizing human potential,"

Brooks said passionately at a recent university strategic planning session. "Too much emphasis has been put on book smarts and technology, and not nearly enough on behavioral science, people smarts, common sense, and leadership development."

Teaching Emotional Intelligence, the awareness of emotions and how we manage these emotions in ourselves and others, would be the foundation for the upcoming coffee meetings. Simple but significant. Brooks reviewed names of students on his class roster one last time, set his alarm, and went to bed. This final act of his life would inspire excellence and growth for an endless bloom.

Chapter 5
Time

William was the first student to meet with Professor Brooks Lambeau at the assigned times at the university coffeehouse. The coffeehouse, decorated with colorful, eclectic art and bicycle parts, was a tourist attraction. The staff were friendly, people smart, and often hired by employers of choice in the area. Brooks was attracted to the hip vibe of the place for years and always felt young at heart meeting there. He couldn't think of many better things in life than good coffee combined with good conversations. Brooks had purchased a dozen T-shirts from the coffeehouse over the years that he wore with pride. His favorite T-shirt read *A MORNING WITHOUT COFFEE IS LIKE...JUST KIDDING, I HAVE NO IDEA.*

"Good morning William," said Brooks. "Your word is TIME. Please record what you wish. But before I forget, I want to give you a gift." Brooks handed over a cloth bag and continued to speak in a warm, melodic tone.

Time is a gift that does not receive the sacredness it deserves. Because time is invisible, it loses respect and our attention. Time is truly all we have in life and it is what we do with this time that shapes our quality of life, our legacy. Time management is the created space to prioritize what we need to do to achieve our dreams and bloom. How we spend our time says a lot about who we are becoming or unbecoming. Who we spend our time with and where we work are some of the biggest decisions of our life. Choose to spend time with people who inspire you to become the best version of yourself. Don't lose precious time worrying too much about what other people think of you. When I was in my 20s as you are, I cared a great deal what people thought of me. In my 40s, I didn't care much what anyone thought of me. Now in my 60s, I've come to the realization that no one was ever thinking of me in the first place!

Intense emotions can quickly transport us into the past or future. Dwelling in the past and foreshadowing the future eliminates the now. Intelligence is successfully managing emotions to be truly present for ourselves and those we lead. Being in the now manifests into presence.

Elite athletes, artists, and leaders possessing optimal presence is commonly referred to as being "in the zone" or "flow." Presence positions one for excellence.

Our world hires and promotes those who demonstrate presence. I have enjoyed being a part of hiring committees for this university and area non-profits because of the immediate positive impact from hiring good people. There has not been a time we hired an administrator or executive who did not demonstrate presence—you could just feel the warm confidence radiate from the individual. This is the "it" factor.

Time, talent, and treasure are paramount to doing good works in the world. However, the greatest gift you can give someone is your time. When you give your time, you give a portion of your life that you will never get back. Three things you cannot recover in life: the opportunity after it's missed, the word after it's spoken, and the time after it's wasted. Time is never wasted on helping another human bloom. Volunteering, mentoring, coaching, and serving others nourishes the human spirit.

You want to know where the most time is wasted? Meetings! I can't tell you how many meetings I have been in where there is no agenda, no objectives, and no actions. Without awareness of the irony, a former boss of mine would say frustratingly, "We are going to keep having meetings until we figure out why no work is getting done." You can't make this stuff up! Your guiding principle when facilitating a meeting is to make sure people's valuable time is not wasted. Here are seven practical tips to run an effective meeting:

1. Have a clear purpose for the meeting.
2. Send out an agenda in advance of the meeting with prioritized objectives.
3. Only invite those that need to be present.
4. Facilitate discussion/decisions that are only needed by the collective group.
5. Keep it less than an hour, if possible.
6. Summarize action steps with individual responsibilities before adjourning the meeting.
7. Have coffee, water, or tea available.

Every meeting has different needs. Adapt accordingly. There is a misconception that long meetings translates into a lot of work getting done. Long meetings are exhausting. Short yet significant should be the goal for every meeting. It's encouraged to cancel scheduled meetings when there is no needed discussion or decisions. Meeting just to meet disengages people unless it is a platform for fellowship. Of the tips I just mentioned, #4 "facilitate discussion/decisions that are only needed by the collective group" deserves the most attention.

Meetings become derailed when two individuals have a sidebar conversation that does not involve the collective group. The two individuals should take their conversation outside the meeting afterwards or at another agreed upon time.

Running effective meetings leads to excellence in workplaces, communities, and beyond and is a huge competitive advantage in business. Most importantly, celebrate the leaders who are stepping up to the challenge to chair committees and run meetings. They are the ones courageously stepping into the arena to make positive change. Show gratitude for all the work that goes into meeting agendas, facilitation, correspondence, and follow-up. You can't complain about meetings until you have the courage to lead some yourself!

Don't lose precious time forecasting how other people will behave in the future. Predicting how people will behave in a future meeting, group project, or at a holiday party often becomes irrational. The reality is, whether good or bad, it never turns out exactly how we think and is mostly false narratives told irrationally by the emotional brain. False narratives make people react irrationally in the present moment to behaviors that exist only in the mind. When you feel this dynamic occurring, activate your logic and ask "Is there evidence that this is true?" There is a good chance there will be no evidence and it is all emotional. Allow the present moment to unfold and adapt accordingly. Don't anticipate, just participate. This will lead to true presence.

Close your eyes and think about time in your life. Waiting for your childhood birthday party? Waiting to see if your middle school crush noticed you? Waiting to see if you were accepted into this university? Waiting…that accelerates time. Never allow waiting to become a habit. Live your dreams and take risks now. The future depends on what you do in the now. Timing will never be absolutely perfect to act. Never avoid doing something, calling it waiting, because you are afraid to fail. All the super good stuff that happened in my life is from the stuff I was almost too scared to do.

Nothing can be achieved yesterday or tomorrow. The past is

gone and the future has not yet arrived. Don't place your self-worth in something that was bad timing. You can meet the right people at the wrong time and the wrong people at the right time. People, places, and purpose don't always gel but when they do watch out because greatness happens. Appreciate these crystallizations on your journey because big magic can be few and far between.

It is healthy to reflect on the past but unhealthy to live there. It is absolutely beneficial to visualize positive future outcomes but do not lose sight of the present to take timely action. Give gratitude for things in real time when you have them. Real time and the opportunity to influence is the five feet in front of our face. It is sad to see how much time is lost in the present moment by people who are too busy looking down at their phones. Looking down at a screen is the thief of real life. Many lose precious time because they are living in the past, waiting for the future, or online with fear of missing out. The only thing you don't want to miss out on is the present moment. That's where the good stuff happens. Time is right here, right now.

Reflection: Where do you spend most of your time? Past? Present? Future? Online?

Chapter 6
Journey

"Good morning Kate," said Brooks. "Your word is JOURNEY. Please record what you wish. But before I forget, I want to give you a gift." Brooks handed over a cloth bag and continued to speak in a warm, melodic tone.

All of humanity is on a unique journey and we do not know the length of the journey. Embrace the journey. Slow down and smell the flowers. A journey to success in life is not a straight line because we learn and receive the most growth during failures, setbacks, and detours. The journey is an adventure of squiggles. Your unique, authentic story is your power. There is no elevator to success, you have to take the stairs and do the work. Do the work in a smart way. You don't have to take the stairs walking backwards. Don't be discouraged when your timing and plan doesn't exactly align with your journey.

Blessings and clarity arrive when we least expect them. There are two important days on your journey—the day you are born and the day you find out why. The third most important day is the day you do something about it! Watch and listen for your why. It will be revealed in your heart. Find the sweet spot which is the intersection of:

- What you love doing
- What you are really good at

- What the world needs
- What you can be paid for

It is human nature to compare ourselves to where others are at on their journey. Shift your focus inward to your own journey because outward comparison robs us of the satisfaction of doing our best with what we have been given. The only comparison should be your own growth from who you were yesterday. This will lead to a unique, colorful bloom.

We put too much pressure on teenagers to decide what they want to do the rest of their lives. Yes, facilitate career exploration and options but to commit to a career when you are 18-years-old is absurd. No wonder why college students are anxious. Some of the test taking can be a head scratcher too. The ACT, SAT, and other tests that rank and place our young adults in colleges does not measure character traits that truly make a difference such as leadership, creativity, self-awareness, compassion, empathy, integrity, courage, resiliency, and relentless work ethic. Just because we can't always test or measure something doesn't mean it shouldn't be boldly taught and valued.

Adults, especially in their 30s and 40s, become anxious because they feel like they cannot abandon what they set out to be at 18-years-old even when feeling complete dissatisfaction in their current situation. A degree earned or craft learned in a specific field should not confine new passions. The journey is about constant experimentation. It's completely okay for high schoolers, college students, young professionals, and beyond to not be 100% certain of what they want to do with the rest of their lives. There are so many opportunities to become something new. Some of the most fascinating people in my life are in their 50s and 60s and still don't know what they want to do with their lives! They wake up continuing to explore.

Seeds are planted along the journey that sprout years later. Focus more on having a growth mindset—endless opportunities to improve. Allow space for pivots, reinvention—and the journey.

People will need to be invested in on their journey. Show you care by providing continuous personal and professional enrichment to bloom. I was talking to a CFO and she concernedly asked me, "What happens if we invest in our people and then they leave the company?" I fired back, "What if you don't and they stay?"

Humans are yearning to be invited on an inspiring journey in the workplace and beyond. Leaders don't force people to follow, they invite them on a journey. An inspiring mission and vision must be established and reinforced daily to all stakeholders. This is the organizational why and required for excellence.

Everybody is on their own journey and it is always changing with new experiences and new transitions. What good is living the life we have been given if all we do is stand in place? People will change on their journey and allow them to do so. Your journey is an original movie that will only be seen from start to finish by you. Many of the most inspiring achievements and contributions to humanity were done by people in their final act. Late bloomers are always a delight!

Giving your best with what you have been given allows you to seize the journey. Focus all your energy on your journey of becoming the best version of you. Many people will help us bloom on our journey. The journey is long, and in the end, it is only with ourselves.

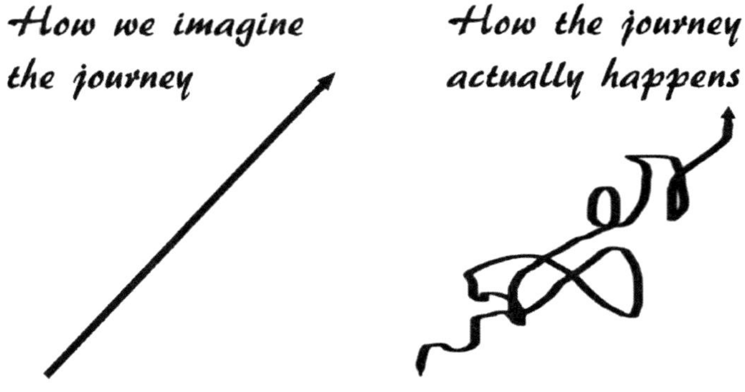

Reflection: What are the most significant events on your journey that have shaped who you are today? What was within your control? What wasn't?

Chapter 7
Dreams

"Good morning Peyton," said Brooks. "Your word is DREAMS. Please record what you wish. But before I forget, I want to give you a gift." Brooks handed over a cloth bag and continued to speak in a warm, melodic tone.

Dreams are the spark to every morning. Dreams get us out of bed and fuel our greatness. The older we become and the more adversity we experience, we lose our dreams that were born in our childhood hearts. Never let go of your dreams and continually revisit what makes you come most alive. We are not old until our regrets outnumber our dreams. Limitations to our dreams only live in our minds. It is all about the vision, not the starting circumstances. We need more dreamers and forward thinkers. There's a reason the front windshield is a lot bigger than the rear view mirror.

High achievers have something in common. They can visualize their dreams with clarity and activate other senses to smell, taste, hear, and feel their dreams. Experiencing their wildest dreams in their mind with emotional connection makes it more real and obtainable.

High achievers have the visual in their mind at all times to guide behavior and bolster discipline. They visualize the excitement of achieving the bloom.

Servant leaders are dream coaches. They inspire the dreams of others. They facilitate the process of helping people find their purpose, their why. Coaching is an ongoing relationship, on or off the court, to inspire others to achieve their dreams and reach their potential. Employers of choice design a culture where servant leaders are in the dream-coaching business. Within this coaching culture, people challenge each other to become the best versions of themselves and to achieve their dreams personally and professionally.

Understanding people's personal and professional dreams brings the human element to the forefront. When you show someone you are invested in their dreams, they will always do more than what is expected. This coaching culture improves engagement and well-being translating into improved productivity. Looking at a person holistically, not as a transactional means to an end, nourishes greatness. Sometimes there is no room for upward mobility within the company. Great leaders launch people outward and upward putting people first. With this approach, there is always a robust pipeline of top talent wanting to join this culture of servant leadership.

There will be critics on your journey when you start achieving your dreams and living your best life. Critics might be battling jealousy, insecurities, or limiting beliefs. Interestingly, they will be the ones standing on the sideline clinging tight to their comfort zone not taking action to help create positive change. Keep pushing forward and courageously showing up for your dreams. Surround yourself with coaches you trust who give you feedback that will position you for success. Don't take criticism from someone you wouldn't ever go to for advice. Big blooms belong to the doers, not critics.

Life will only change when one becomes more committed to

their dreams than their comfort zone. Every morning you have two choices—continue to sleep with your dreams or wake up and chase them. As long as you are breathing it is never too late to dream a new dream. **Playing small serves no one—dream BIG and share your gifts with the world!** Our world needs BIG blooms.

Reflection: What is your biggest dream personally and professionally? Is it BIG enough? What steps can you take toward achieving it?

Chapter 8
In the Garden

Gardening brought Brooks peace of mind from all the hustle and bustle of life. Brooks had created a robust garden in his backyard over the years. It was a hobby turned into a passion. It is in the garden where wisdom often came to Brooks from high above.

Most of what Brooks ate came fresh from his garden. Onions, carrots, herbs, tomatoes, cucumbers, lettuce, and radishes were in the garden. These foods were the fuel to his positive energy. In recent years, Brooks added vibrant flowers to his garden. "Our world would be a lot better place if everyone first focused on improving their own garden," Brooks said once at a conference.

Kneeling next to the flowers, bare hands massaging the rich soil, Brooks began to practice mindfulness. The garden is where Brooks strengthened his mindfulness most to utilize in all areas of his life. Massaging the soil, he transformed himself in the moment noticing his breathing, the patterns in the dirt, the smell and texture of the flowers, and his thoughts. With each dig and swipe of the dirt, Brooks could feel the cooler temperatures of the soil. At times, Brooks would become intensely present in the moment forgetting he was in his own backyard. There was much to experience within the garden as long as one slowed down to pay attention. Brooks practiced this mindfulness too when eating.

Brooks noticed the flower he had been nourishing diligently for quite some time in full bloom looking healthy and strong. This particular flower struggled growing, unlike the other flowers. It was more faded than the others but was still holding on. Brooks gave this flower extra attention nourishing it with the right doses of water, plant food, shade, and sunlight. Once the right environment was created, the flower finally bloomed like all the others. "Humans are not much different than flowers," Brooks thought kneeling next to the flowers. "Every human needs special attention, coaching, and love to fully bloom. Humans have remarkable potential for positive growth at any age and during any season."

Seeing growth in all aspects of life, both in humanity and his garden, brought Brooks joy. Brooks observed an emerging trend of artificial flowers and real flowers. Artificial flowers being artificial intelligence, technology, and automation. Real flowers being humans. Artificial flowers serve a purpose for efficiency, convenience, and processing big data. Real flowers, humans, serve a purpose for authentic leadership, compassion, and inspiring others to bloom. "As technology continues to accelerate, so will the need to become even more human," Brooks whispered to himself. "There is nothing more wasted than a human becoming artificial and robotic."

Brooks lifted himself from his knees and started to head back towards the house as the sun rays peeked through the trees. It was a beautiful late afternoon. Brooks stopped halfway to the house and turned back to look at the flowers with appreciation. Bright colors of yellow, pink, purple, red, orange, blue, and green were in full bloom. The colors reminded Brooks a lot of the emotions he feels. Red reminded him of anger but also love. Yellow reminded him of trust and friendship. Blue of sadness and grief. Purple of faith and renewal. Green of surprise and fear. His vast emotions, just like the vast colors, made him feel human and alive.

Now back inside his house, Brooks heard his music still playing in the living room. He walked over to turn the music off but noticed Van Morrison – In The Garden was playing. He kept it on, turning up the soulful song.

Chapter 9
Action

"Good morning Kelly," said Brooks. "Your word is ACTION. Please record what you wish. But before I forget, I want to give you a gift." Brooks handed over a cloth bag and continued to speak in a warm, melodic tone.

Action puts dreams and goals into motion. I have observed an overwhelming number of students and professionals aspire greatness but never act. They have a false narrative that there will be a perfect time. The kryptonite to action is the word "after" and is often used as an excuse for inaction. I hear people say "after" and it is like they are putting another brick on the wall between them and their dreams. I will do it after I get the new job. I will do it after the kids leave the house. I will do it after I retire. I will do it after I lose weight. We will launch the new product after this year. It goes on and on and on. Action is right here, right now.

Action in the now is what manifests perfect timing. One of the brilliant brand slogans of all time is "Just Do It." Simple yet significant. Self-reflection is valuable as long as one does not create a poor habit of overthinking that it paralyzes the doing. Behavioral science sheds light on the fact that excellence begs for motion—potential energy to kinetic energy. Your core values—are they on the walls or in the halls? Leadership is core values in action—in the halls in every interaction.

The great leaders create an entrepreneurial culture where team members feel empowered to make decisions, without fear of being reprimanded for failure. Failure is part of creativity and innovation in a growth mindset culture. It is astonishing how many organizations lose time and money spending days thinking, analyzing, rethinking, reanalyzing, and scheduling excessive, lethargic meetings without ever putting anything into action. Action eats excuses for breakfast. Under the surface, this culture has a fear of failure and a lack of leadership. Meanwhile, the competition is passing by in the fast lane with action and when they do fail, they fail fast forward.

Imperfect action is better than perfect inaction—analysis paralysis. Don't get too absorbed in the thinking, saying, and dreaming that you forget the doing. The value is in the work, the action. I've observed people listening to a podcast a day and reading a book a week, but unfortunately they never put the learning into action. Consumed knowledge and strategy needs to be released. You can be a lifelong learner but without action there will be no bloom. Success is the intersection of acquiring knowledge and skills—and then most importantly putting them into action. Great leaders inspire action and accountability.

Adversity accelerates action. I have seen brilliant creativity and inventiveness at times of adversity. Crises accelerate innovation and unity. Illnesses accelerate priorities. Adversity is a good thing when there is a positive response and a "can do" attitude present. When there is no urgency or inspiring vision, things become idle and too comfortable. Comfort creates lethargic behavior.

Actions create emotions. When we feel and embrace negative emotions, we have the choice to remain with them or shift away from them to a positive state by taking action. This is personal accountability and liberty at its finest. Act differently to change a thought and feeling. Act as if you are becoming your ideal self. Doing the same thing over and over and expecting different results is the definition of insanity. Feeling lethargic? Exercise. Feeling down? Volunteer in the community or buy the person behind you a cup of coffee. Lacking confidence? Stand tall. Consumed with worry? Pray.

Excuses and complaining fertilize the weeds. Complaining without offering a solution is called whining! Excuses paralyze us from the simplicity of it all—just show up. Just showing up is the starting point to all action. Just show up to your family, your work, your teammates, your clients, your community, and your promises. Don't wait for the perfect time because you will wait forever. Great leaders don't tell you what to do or make excuses, they show you how it is done by how they lead their life. Without question, great leaders lead by example. When something goes wrong, they start with themselves. It is small actions done with repetition and discipline that shapes our bloom.

After one of my talks at a symposium, a human resources director of a large company approached me and asked if it were possible for his workplace not to have a culture.

I was startled by the question and immediately thought of all the employees who must be similarly confused getting up in the morning and going to a place that has no established culture. If senior leadership was confused and not aligned, they surely would be too. Leaders inspire and motivate the why for coming to work. More importantly, servant leaders coach people to find their individual why.

The question isn't whether your workplace has a culture or not. You can't not have a culture. The question is—is the culture by default or is the culture by design? Servant leaders use action to design, inspire, and protect the culture every single day. If you don't use intentional action to design culture it happens by default and strays from core values—and the mission and vision. Culture is the result of the poorest behavior leaders are willing to tolerate. Great leaders protect culture and do not allow unacceptable behaviors. Culture is the combination of what you design and what you allow. Inaction for unacceptable behaviors will spread negativity and toxicity like wildfire throughout a culture! Servant leaders design a people-first culture to drive results and they consistently hold all people accountable to the same standards and values regardless of title, experience, or personality. Top talent with growth mindsets will not settle for anything less than deliberately designed cultures as they strive for excellence.

Cultures are not only in workplaces but also in our homes. Likewise, households can have minimal design and this leads to dysfunction and passive living. Choose to actively design your life to achieve your dreams and vision—and share your gifts with the world.

?

Reflection: What immediate action is needed in your life to achieve your dreams? What should you no longer push off until tomorrow? Is your culture and life by design or by default?

Chapter 10
Self-Awareness

"Good morning Craig," said Brooks. "Your word is SELF-AWARENESS. Please record what you wish. But before I forget, I want to give you a gift." Brooks handed over a cloth bag and continued to speak in a warm, melodic tone.

There has been a clear pattern throughout my years teaching, coaching, and consulting. The people that push off Emotional Intelligence as rubbish, or too soft, are the ones who need it the most. There is self-deception to protect the ego. The people that think they are done learning and growing have the biggest gap to close on the journey to becoming the best version of themselves.

Too many people are offended when their thinking is simply challenged. We need increased self-awareness to tend the garden for more respectful disagreements. We need more self-awareness and adaptability to prevent emotional reactions to everything said to us.

Self-awareness is the discipline to be in tune with our thoughts and feelings that are always changing. Monitoring self-talk. Watching judgments, biases, impulses, and assumptions. Conscious reflection. Self-awareness is the ability to monitor, in real time, what we can and cannot control. Paying attention to our attention in the now.

Without self-awareness, the emotional brain can run wild in digital correspondence. For example, think of sending a text and not receiving a response within several hours. The emotional brain goes nuts! Thoughts such as "What's wrong?" or "Did I say something wrong?" or "Are they ok?" irrationally hijacks us. In reality, the person on the receiving end of the text is out enjoying the afternoon kayaking the river without their phone. Think of how often these scenarios play out in any given day, and how much precious time is lost being emotionally hijacked and out of reality. Keep close observation on how technology use and consuming media impacts your well-being. Media has become increasingly more fake and recklessly produces irrational fear. Unfortunately, some people's whole lives are consumed by text, email, and social media. They are like robots.

Common sense is the most valued and respected intelligence in all of mankind. One can easily practice using common sense by being more aware and reflecting on situations before making decisions. To pause, assess, and reassess in an ever-changing world. We can't control events and other people's behaviors but we can always control how we choose to respond to shape the outcome. There is great freedom in always being able to choose our response with confidence, composure, and grace. Create pause to reframe thoughts. Create space to realize positive intent and your approach, and worldview, will become more graceful.

On a deeper level, self-awareness is the ability to authentically know ourselves. To know our strengths, weaknesses, dreams, and journey. To know our life story and to have the ability to articulate how our life story and all the good and bad experiences have shaped our current beliefs, behaviors, and worldview. This level of self-awareness reveals our real self. An accurate, reality-based self-assessment is the starting point to positive growth. One can only achieve becoming an ideal self once the real self is clearly established and understood. The best mentors and coaches compassionately facilitate self-awareness in others.

You can measure deep self-awareness by the ease of which an individual can articulate their life story and beyond. Peel the onion back nonjudgmentally on your life, your parents' life, their parents' life, and so on. Awareness of this rich timeline of trials and triumph informs you on the "why" of your perceptions, beliefs, worldview, and more. This is all part of your life painting. You might uncover poverty, war, racism, tragedy, depression, addiction, or abuse. You will see victories of love, resilience, faith, and courage. Why people act the way they do will crystallize and how it influenced your childhood. You will become self-aware of the start of your brushstroke, your journey, within an endless painting. This will shed light on your life story and give you the freedom to choose what ongoing cycles you want to break. For example, limiting beliefs that people who are wealthy are greedy or crooks. Hard-earned wealth is perfectly okay—when you bloom you will receive abundance! With wealth comes the opportunity for generosity. Everyone needs to zoom out and do this family exploration to truly bloom. On a macro-level, our society needs to come together with compassion and collectively do this. Honestly looking at history to inspire progress and positive change.

Self-awareness is the building block to live our best lives. A life without self-awareness never blooms. Ego gets in the way of true self-awareness. Denial persists. Ego attempts to bury weaknesses to protect itself. People commonly do not want to admit their weaknesses, their blind spots. Exceptional leaders can look in the mirror and be brutally honest with themselves and their life story. Sharing strengths is easy. Anybody can do that. However, exceptional leaders can share their weaknesses openly too without losing a drop of confidence. People are attracted to and trust others who own their blind spots with humility.

Play to your strengths. Knowing and leveraging our strengths is the path to satisfaction in work and life. Continue to fertilize your strengths and encourage others to do so too. Servant leaders do this by putting people in positions to be successful based on their strengths.

Lack of self-awareness leads to missed opportunities to lead, serve, and inspire. More times than not, dysfunctional behaviors in workplaces and homes are because of emotional wounds that have not been dealt with positively or at all. The dysfunction is deeply rooted in the past and has nothing to do with current colleagues, partners, or culture. People who have not yet done the inner work projecting their pain on to the world will need transformational leadership and coaching. Poor leadership and dysfunctional behavior is only a symptom from emotional wounds. Emotional wounds referring to any event that negatively impacted one's well-being in their lifetime. Some type of unjust emotional hurt or pain inflicted. A derogatory comment or unprofessional experience that burned an emotional scar in psyche at a subconscious level that freezes the bloom years later. Someone you fully trusted dropping the ball. Limiting beliefs. The best leaders do the inner work and have coaches to guide the process to get to the root cause.

We all have weaknesses and wounds because we are human. Life can be messy. The very best surround themselves with people who strengthen their blind spots in life. Self-awareness is an ongoing journey and takes courage and vulnerability to see our authentic selves warts and all. The process of self-discovery is so worth it. Do the inner work to become the best version of you.

Intentional observation of the present moment without trying to modify it is called mindfulness. Mindfulness is a form of self-awareness and is an excellent way to manage stress, anxiety, and burnout. It is a discipline to regain focus, confidence, and clarity. Our minds can become like a shaken snow globe with stress, uncertainty, and never ending to-do lists—restless monkey mind. One of my favorite tools which I have used most of my life is called Rose, Thorn, Bud. Practicing self-awareness, start monitoring your **Rose, Thorn, Bud** daily as much as possible. Two opportunistic times to do this is during transition periods on your way to class or work and on your way home—and mini-moments of solitude throughout your day.

ROSE: A highlight, success, or something positive that happened. (Gratitude)

THORN: A challenge you experienced or something that is stressful that you could use help and support with. (Humility)

BUD: A positive opportunity developing or something exciting that might happen. (Growth)

Rose, Thorn, Bud is a popular teaching within our family science courses because of the positive impact on kids' emotional health too. Parents, school teachers, and counselors love Rose, Thorn, Bud because it teaches our youth self-awareness and significantly reduces their stress and anxiety while building strong emotional health. An amazing benefit of asking kids Rose, Thorn, Bud is that it gives one an empathic bridge into their world. Do this exercise often anytime, anywhere.

Reflection: What are your strengths and blind spots? Can you easily articulate your life story and how it has shaped your worldview and leadership style? What is your current Rose, Thorn, Bud?

Chapter 11
Clarity

"Good morning Michelle," said Brooks. "Your word is CLARITY. Please record what you wish. But before I forget, I want to give you a gift." Brooks handed over a cloth bag and continued to speak in a warm, melodic tone.

Clarity allows us to make good decisions with confidence that are in alignment with our core values and dreams. As self-awareness improves, so does clarity. The more clarity we have the easier decision making becomes—clarity gives us confidence to say "No" and "Not now." Confident people decline things that do not move the needle towards their priorities, passions, dreams, and goals. Be mindful of how constant people pleasing creates fatigue and disappointment. I respect people who say "No" and "Not now" because it demonstrates clarity and ambitions. Clarity helps us avoid drama. Emotions are highly contagious. Drama attracts and fertilizes drama. Positivity attracts and fertilizes positivity.

Noise, dark alleys, and unhealthy habits cloud our clarity. Unfortunately, some students misbelieve that the most creative and inspired artists do their best work under the influence. Ask the best of the best and they will tell you their greatest work was achieved sober with clarity. Bad habits put a suffocating frost on the bloom.

Awareness of emotional triggers will position you to have

calm and clarity when others are reacting. We cannot manage anything that we are not aware is happening. Self-awareness of natural tendencies to emotional triggers is essential for responding with clarity instead of reacting irrationally. Emotional triggers can be deep rooted. For example, someone who did not receive attention as a child might start yelling when they feel they aren't being heard. A person who did not receive love and nurturing as a child most likely will feel more insecure and inadequate. A person physically or emotionally controlled in the past could very well overreact when being directed to complete a simple task. Feeling insecure for being short can cause an individual to overcompensate and act aggressive or arrogant to become psychologically "tall." This dynamic is everywhere in life and is most prevalent when people do not have clarity of their innermost emotional triggers.

Everybody has intense emotional triggers. You should see me when I see Oreo cheesecake! Triggers are not only formed from past experiences but also when beliefs and passions are challenged. Politics. Religion. Fandom. Being taught to avoid talking about politics and religion has led to an unhealthy gap between the differing vantage points. We need to learn and embrace Emotional Intelligence to have respectful dialogue on difficult topics. The absence of open and civil dialogue of these polarizing topics has led to raising our voice and not our curiosity when conversations eventually happen. Ignorance manifests. It is rain that grows flowers, not thunder. Emotional Intelligence is needed for the families, workplaces, and communities that want to thrive and achieve excellence. The key is to be self-aware of triggers so they can be observed and managed with clarity.

People who achieve their big dreams and inspire others to do the same have excellent clarity. They practice mindfulness and are constantly tending the garden of their thoughts and feelings.

Taking mini-moments each day for meditation, monitoring our breaths with intention, and appreciating the natural world around us improves clarity. Clarity is boosted naturally with exercise. The more positive habits you have going on in your life, the more clarity you will have. One feeds off the other and you will experience how success breeds success. A clear mind and pure heart puts us in position to truly bloom.

Reflection: What values, behaviors, and types of people give you the most clarity? What habits, behaviors, and types of people cloud your ability to think clearly? What are your natural emotional triggers?

Chapter 12
Heroes

"Good morning Ben," said Brooks. "Your word is HEROES. Please record what you wish. But before I forget, I want to give you a gift." Brooks handed over a cloth bag and continued to speak in a warm, melodic tone.

Heroes will change for you over the course of your life. When you are a small child, your hero is the baker behind the counter who hands you your favorite chocolate doughnut. When you are a teenager, your heroes are pop stars, celebrities, and professional athletes. But as you mature, new heroes appear. There is a new gratitude for true heroes—doctors, nurses, and those on the frontlines who take care of us and our loved ones. Parents, spouses, and family who stand by our side through thick and thin. Our police officers, firefighters, and military who keep us safe and protected. The plumber who is a volunteer EMT. Farmers, food manufacturers, and grocery stores that provide us quality food. Teachers who inspire and nourish our children's future. True heroes, we learn, are ordinary people living in our communities doing extraordinary things.

My little brother Jimmy was a wild kid in his teenage years. He gave mom and dad a lot of heartburn with his drinking and drugs. It was hard to watch because he was smart and no one wanted to see such a brilliant mind be wasted.

Jimmy didn't go to college and I think that's when a lot of people wrote him off. We all go through those turbulent teenage years I would think to myself watching from an optimistic vantage point. And college isn't for everybody. I would here people talk negatively about him in the community and how he was such a loser. But I knew the potential in my little brother and that's all that mattered. Our family prayed for Jimmy. I continuously challenged him to be his own hero.

Jimmy turned his life around and quit drinking, doing drugs, and getting into trouble. Over time, he became respected in New York as a firefighter, servant leader, and had a beautiful wife and two small baby girls. Jimmy received the prestigious "Community Volunteer of the Year Award" by the chamber of commerce. He was a thriving late bloomer!

On a September morning, Jimmy died saving lives running into a burning tower as a firefighter during a terrorist attack in New York City. He not only became a hero in our small hometown but an American hero. I knew he could be a hero before anyone else did.

Reflection: Who has made the greatest positive impact on you in your life? What are this individual's top attributes? Have you let them know?

Chapter 13
A Doctor Visit

The morning coffee meetings were going better than expected. Brooks was surprised by the prompt attendance and inspiring conversations. He could tell a lot about students' potential by their curiosity and willingness to learn.

Brooks was now back at the university hospital waiting for his appointment time. He was wearing a worn vintage T-shirt that read *LIFE'S A GARDEN, DIG IT.* The hospital had world-class care and this was apparent with interactions Brooks had with his doctors. His doctors had a warm confidence. He had heard past horror stories of doctors elsewhere being cold, robotic, and lacking the human touch. His doctors were brilliant both with medical expertise and Emotional Intelligence. On a human level, the frontline all the way up to the doctors were approachable and accessible.

Sitting in the hospital atrium, Brooks was observing the good number of people waiting for their appointments just like him. People were reading magazines. Mindlessly scrolling phones. Daydreaming. One woman was clearly pregnant. Brooks continued scanning the people waiting. One young man was bald and appeared to be receiving chemotherapy. Another man looked happy as if a family member had just received good news. Others looked exhausted. "People and their families are experiencing highs and lows in health all the time and this enters our workplaces," Brooks thought. "People are scared, tired, and beautifully hopeful. We need to be boldly human in our leadership."

Although it was part of his terminal illness, Brooks had immense gratitude for his health care experience. With elegance, his doctors explained complex medical terminology in ways that were easily understood. The emotional care was impressive. His doctors had a profound adaptability between head and heart that gave Brooks comfort in his circumstance. "These bedside manners are vital for leadership in all industries, not only health care," Brooks thought while his doctor stepped out of the room. "There is magic when people know how to adapt quickly between head and heart."

The doctor visit went well. Brooks was still dying but at least he was in the presence of world-class compassionate care.

Chapter 14
Adaptability

"Good morning Erin," said Brooks. "Your word is ADAPTABILITY. Please record what you wish. But before I forget, I want to give you a gift." Brooks handed over a cloth bag and continued to speak in a warm, melodic tone.

Adaptability liberates us to continue on our journey and begin new every morning. Not utilizing self-awareness limits us from adapting to ever-changing situations, people, and opportunities all around us. There are two levels to adaptability. The first being interpersonal adaptability in real time to changing emotions. This is the communication skill differentiating the mediocre professionals from the All-Stars. All-Stars have self-awareness to determine what needs to be activated between head and heart. They also have self-management to switch back-and-forth between head and heart on-demand. Using our head is necessary for disarming emotional hijacks, ego, false narratives, and irrational thoughts. Asking oneself "where is there evidence that this is true?" Being rational is part of exceptional leadership. Logic is required.

Great leaders do not react based on emotion alone and this inspires calm, clarity, and trust within their teams. However, we must also connect with heart. Knowing when and where is fundamental to Emotional Intelligence. I have worked with people who are on autopilot with zero adaptability between head and heart. This lack of adaptability translates into only leading with the head—logical but cold, or only leading with the heart—compassionate but irrational.

Servant leaders continuously adapt back-and-forth between head and heart to successfully lead themselves and others. They follow their heart but take their brains with them. At times, we need to lead with our gut. The intuitive core. You can have all the data you want in your head and love in your heart but sometimes you have to trust how you feel intuitively and act on it. The best decisions I make are when there is alignment with my head, heart, and core—a full body yes or no.

Adaptability needs discipline with changing emotions and needs all around us. Authentically connect human to human. Master adaptability between head, heart, and core and your relationships personally and professionally will bloom. This adaptability is boldly human leadership.

I like the golden rule of treating everybody how *you'd* like to be treated. I love the platinum rule of treating everybody how *they'd* like to be treated. The platinum rule focuses on understanding and serving others' emotions. If we treat everybody how we'd like to be treated as the golden rule suggests, we are not going to be able to successfully adapt to the dynamic personalities and needs immediately surrounding us. Healthy, trusting relationships bloom when we adapt to treat people how they'd like to be treated.

Treating others how they'd like to be treated takes curiosity as well as adaptive leadership. Think of all the different ways people like to be treated. For example, an introvert would appreciate a quiet, low energy approach.

An extrovert, or social butterfly, would appreciate more energy. An employee might appreciate a sincere "super job this week—you're amazing" more than a small gift or other recognition. Awareness of personality types of those in your life is the bridge to adaptive servant leadership. Understand the love languages of those you lead and serve—especially your spouse if you marry! Awareness of unique human interests is the bridge to inclusive leadership. Adaptability is at the core of successful and meaningful interactions with others.

Think of all the things that interest you. Now, what if I told you that only 20% of your colleagues have those exact same interests? Does this change what you talk about? Does this change the questions you ask? Yes, certainly. This makes you want to adapt to build better connections. We can become self-absorbed in our own personality, interests, hobbies, and life that we never pause to treat others how they want to be treated. Wilting relationships are self-serving. Relationships that bloom have empathy and have the ability to put oneself in another's shoes, another's world. True emotional connection happens when adapting to the unique interests of those in our presence. The rich stories below the surface connects humanity.

Last April, I was speaking at a SHRM conference in Chicago and speaking directly to the importance of the platinum rule on successfully adapting to different people. After my talk, a human resources manager came up to me to say hello. This man was relieved and thankful for my message. "Thank you so much for speaking on adaptability to the different personalities and emotions all around us," he told me. "My boss is always telling us 'I don't know what everyone's problem is, I treat everybody the same.'"

This looks good on paper but is ineffective. Yes, be in alignment with core values but treat everybody how they want to be treated. Adapting to the continuum of emotions in real time engages humanity. Authentic adaptability builds trust and capacity to serve. You become a servant leader when you realize that life is about what you give rather than what you get.

The second level of adaptability is the long game focused on big transitions in business and life. This level is continuously adapting with a growth mindset on our journey. Growth mindsets—believing there are endless opportunities to improve oneself and others—are the best employees, teammates, and friends. There is always room for improvement and a better way. The art of letting go of limiting beliefs is required for new beginnings to bloom. Holding on to the past and avoiding change is the source of a lot of self-inflicted pain in business—and life. Old ways won't open new doors. The seven most expensive words in business are *WE HAVE ALWAYS DONE IT THAT WAY.* Problems don't cease, they just change. Most things are temporary and fluid. Life throws curveballs and we must successfully pivot, reinvent—and adapt on our journey.

I've taught at this campus for years and the person that comes to mind who is the very best at adaptability is not a Ph.D. The person is Wes, the janitor. Wes has high Emotional Intelligence. People gravitate towards Wes. People trust Wes. People like how approachable he is. I love watching from a distance how he can chat with all walks of life on campus. He adapts gracefully from introverted students to extroverted faculty. He adapts quickly to students celebrating excellent exam scores to students who feel defeated after failing exams. He adapts to how people tick and their interests, area of study, and hobbies.

Wes adapts to people because he knows that is how he can truly connect with others. He treats others how they want to be treated. He is like a chameleon to all the emotions around him to make those in his presence comfortable. People love him for his adaptive leadership and approachable personality. He would be an excellent executive if he didn't love our university and his job so much. Someday, mark my words, there will be a statue on this campus to honor Wes's life!

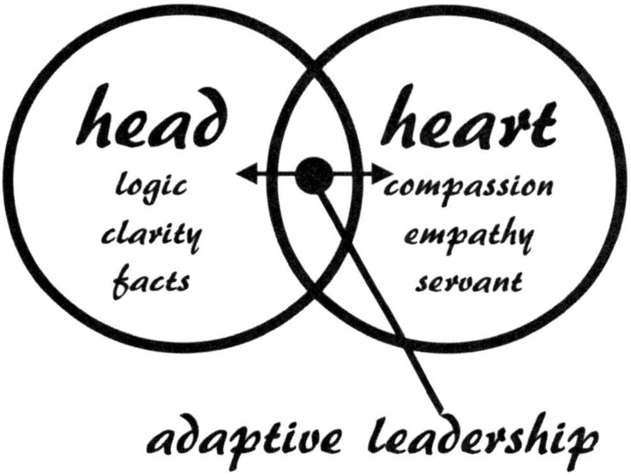

Reflection: When have you needed to lead more with your head? Your heart? Your gut? All three at once? What actions could you start taking now to apply the platinum rule and treat others as they would like to be treated?

Chapter 15
Empathy

"Good morning Emily," said Brooks. "Your word is EMPATHY. Please record what you wish. But before I forget, I want to give you a gift." Brooks handed over a cloth bag and continued to speak in a warm, melodic tone.

One cannot successfully lead, serve, and inspire without empathy. Empathy is the ability to put ourselves in another's shoes and the curiosity to understand someone else's story and perspective. Empathy is the healthy way to look at others' lives and is genuine, nonjudgmental curiosity. Empathy is the gateway to servant leadership and authentic human connection. Healthy cultures have empathy. Suspending our ego by putting ourselves in another person's shoes is magical human connection and leads to a culture of trust and teamwork—an environment for thriving creativity and innovation. Empathy is the ultimate action to treat the diversity of humanity with dignity. Exceptional leaders have empathy. **People will forget a lot of things in life but they will never forget how you made them feel.**

Diverse thinking is the byproduct of diverse life stories and the spark to creativity and innovation. Empathy is scanning for, observing, and celebrating diverse thinking. Six plus three equals nine. But so does five plus four. The way you do things isn't always the only way to do them. Respect other people's way of thinking and perspective. All voices need to be heard and all angles considered. Empathy is seeing with the eyes of another, listening with the ears of another, and feeling with the heart of another. The great leaders fertilize empathy.

To develop empathetic leadership, we must understand time. Time distances us from who we once were in our own life and historic societal events. To successfully lead and coach others, we have to remember how we felt and behaved at different periods of our lives. This is hard to do because interpreting how we would have behaved in the past is based on our current beliefs, wisdom, and situation. We erroneously say, "I would have never done that!" when often we did, multiple times. The best parents, mentors, and coaches have empathy to transport themselves in time to who they once were at a key life stage. Do you remember what it was like for you as a teenager in a constant peer-pressure environment? Do seasoned professionals remember what it was like as a young professional fresh out of college trying to navigate appropriate workplace norms and behaviors? Do senior executives remember what it was like to lead their first team feeling the immense duty for helping people grow in their careers? Empathy is critical for transporting ourselves through time to remember emotionally where we once were and putting ourselves in others' shoes to effectively lead, serve, and inspire.

Sympathy and empathy are different. Sympathy is feeling *for* someone, empathy is feeling *with* someone. Empathy is much more powerful. A good friend of mine, Manny, is a sales executive. He is what every professional should strive to become—a trusted advisor. Manny has built a highly successful sales career with empathetic selling. He is an incredible relationship builder and listener, and is always asking great questions. Nothing is assumed or forecasted before meeting with a customer. He feels with his customers, understanding their unique pain points and challenges. One size fits one.

Manny never sells anything that does not truly benefit his customers. Honesty and integrity are part of Manny's DNA and this is why he is trusted. Manny delivers customized solutions for customer challenges and if he does not have a great fit, he will suggest other resources to serve his customers. Manny, a servant leader, uses empathy for customer service excellence.

I'll never forget my honeymoon in Hawaii when my wife and I did SNUBA together in the ocean. SNUBA, which is an acronym for Surface Nexus Underwater Breathing Apparatus, allows for your air tube to be connected to a raft that floats nearby on the surface of the water. Our SNUBA excursion was close to shore on Kauai Island right next to the Beach House Restaurant which has amazing cuisine and even more amazing sunsets. The air tube allows for about a 25-foot deep exploration so you can easily experience the presence of aqua life while having the peace of mind that you can return to the raft above surface for normal breathing. Above the surface water, you would never know the vibrant aqua life several feet below. We were amazed of the diverse, colorful fish and life below the surface with each dive into the water. Exact same body of water just above and below the surface.

This experience, like activities surrounded by nature often do, reminded me of the power of empathy. We can look at a human being and judge their entire life above the surface with one mental snapshot. Gender, skin color, and appearance is all above the surface. Superficial. We must go below the surface, underwater, and truly get to know and understand a person. There is an intriguing story below the surface in every human—including ourselves! The best way to go below the surface is by asking thoughtful questions and empathetically listening. Thriving organizations form deep emotional connection with all stakeholders. Servant leaders express attentive interest in others. They are curious to know others' story and determine if they can be a resource on the journey.

Servant leaders search and listen with empathy for ways to serve.

Look at a picture of an iceberg above and below the water surface. Powerful. This iceberg image is one of my favorites and has been in all my offices since graduating college. The iceberg reminds me daily of Emotional Intelligence inwardly and outwardly. Self-awareness doing the inner work below the surface. Empathy authentically connecting socially below the surface. Healthy, trusting relationships being below the surface. All the good stuff is below the surface made possible with Emotional Intelligence!

The iceberg is also an excellent reminder of what success really looks like. We see success above the surface in servant leaders, professional athletes, musicians, and so on all of the time and it makes it look easy—we only see the glamor. What we don't see is all the hard work, training, learning, failure, discipline, rejection, and risk below the surface. People want to take your spot until they realize what it takes to play your position! To be the best you have to do the work below the surface. There are no shortcuts to excellence.

Exceptional leaders have group empathy. I call this "Empathy 2.0." Group empathy goes beyond interpersonal emotions and monitors organizational emotions. The great leaders can feel the pulse of the organization, and their community, in real time. They can feel the culture and whether it is shifting for better or worse. Exceptional leaders with Empathy 2.0 can see how teams and departments of the entire organization fit together like pieces in a puzzle. There is good judgment on how people will work together based on personalities, strengths, weaknesses, experience, and even sub-cultures. With curiosity, these leaders go below the surface to see how everybody is interconnected to support the mission and vision. Group empathy is achieved with social awareness by scanning team dynamics and asking pulse check questions throughout the organization. Asking good questions brings reality and meaning to observations, connecting the dots. Great leaders continuously ask great questions. The excellent cultures are more horizontal than vertical where all feel empowered to influence positive change. Because of this astute social awareness, servant leaders are able to place people in positions to be successful and thrive. As an organization expands, so does the demand for Empathy 2.0.

I've observed that people have a hard time with empathy because they can't give their full attention. They become distracted by looking at their phone, email, or elsewhere while someone is talking. Digital obesity. Being rude. Fear of missing out. Whatever you want to call it. The start of empathetic human connection is eye contact and undivided attention. Learn to listen without interruption and you'll hear amazing things! Good door opener questions are "Tell me more" and "Talk more about that." Silence is important to truly listen and understand. Empathetic responses include "It sounds to me like…" "What I hear you saying…" "Did I understand that correctly?" Blooming relationships, whether personal or professional, go below the surface. The inspiring coffee meetings with colleagues and the romantic date nights with your lover have no phones and full human attention.

Reflection: What questions can you ask to go below the surface to truly get to know and serve others? How have you falsely judged someone and what did you learn from this?

Chapter 16
Curiosity

"Good morning Vijay," said Brooks. "Your word is CURIOSITY. Please record what you wish. But before I forget, I want to give you a gift." Brooks handed over a cloth bag and continued to speak in a warm, melodic tone.

Curiosity is childlike wonder that we should carry in our minds, hearts, and souls throughout life. Children explore, play, create, and ask questions with constant curiosity. Play is the original form of research and ignites creativity and innovation. We are designed to be naturally curious—to experiment and play. Curiosity is the spark behind the spark of every great idea. I've always inspired curiosity and experimentation in my teaching and found that this accelerates enthusiasm for learning and growth.

The fear of failure is very human. Great leaders create an environment to learn quickly from failure and to continue to be courageously curious. After failures, we must continue onward to tinker, question, and experiment. The role of a leader is not to have all the brilliant ideas and answers. The great leaders create a stage to convene curiosity, experimentation, and ideas—and then take a step back.

In my advising business, one of my main goals in working with companies and organizations chasing excellence is to create an entrepreneurial culture. Entrepreneurs are naturally curious and self-starters which drives organizational excellence—and growth. Instead of having a top-down structure, an entrepreneurial culture should be created within the company encouraging all to think like an entrepreneur and change agent. This is empowering! A really good employee treats the business as if it were his or her own. This entrepreneurial mindset inspires thoughtful decisions, accountability, and continuous improvement. Hire an entrepreneurial attitude, train skill.

In a dream world, every person should be self-employed for a solid year. Being self-employed quickly makes you appreciate all the moving parts of a business. You carefully watch money spent and become more resourceful. You intimately meet risk and reward. You focus on the customer experience. Every employee should learn the entrepreneurial spirit. Also, entrepreneurs are constantly seeking feedback. They are continuously asking "What went well?" and "What could have gone better?" Asking curious questions, driven by the entrepreneurial spirit, breaks down defensiveness and leads to continuous improvement. It also leads to success personally and professionally. Entrepreneurial cultures collectively have ongoing feedback loops. One of my favorite and brilliantly simple curiosity feedback loops is **Start, Stop, Continue.**

Start: What should we start doing?

Stop: What should we stop doing?

Continue: What should we continue doing that is currently working well?

It is sad to see adults lose their childlike wonder and curiosity. They conform to small thinking, trivial rules, and black and white options only—our life is full of magnificent color! Their minds become fixed like cement. The best professionals color outside the lines and are self-starters. They speak up on projects. Not hiding, they have courage to say "I have an idea" and "Here is where I believe we can improve." They challenge the status quo. Servant leaders create safe space where all feel comfortable to voice their ideas and curiosity. Engagement soars and people feel tremendously valued.

Curiosity amplifies empathy because it gives us compassionate tenacity to want to understand others. Life is a process of creation and the future belongs to the curiously creative. A sign of intelligence is that you are constantly wondering, questioning, and curious.

Reflection: When, if ever, did you lose your childlike wonder? Why? How can you have more of an entrepreneurial mindset? What should you start, stop, and continue?

Chapter 17
Confidence

"Good morning Justin," said Brooks. "Your word is CONFIDENCE. Please record what you wish. But before I forget, I want to give you a gift." Brooks handed over a cloth bag and continued to speak in a warm, melodic tone.

Confidence illuminates our best selves. Confidence is an internal belief and the way we use our God-given abilities to show up and serve others in the world. External validation is unnecessary for true confidence. Confidence isn't walking into a room thinking you are better than everyone, it's walking into a room not having to compare yourself to anyone at all. The inner belief is all that matters. The inner belief, self-esteem, that you can achieve it and deserve it. Unfortunately, humans seek external validation from others for confidence and self-worth the majority of their lifetime. Parents. Family. Bosses. Peers. Social media. The firm decision to no longer need external validation for self-worth is the single greatest game changer to enjoying life!

Self-compassion and daily discipline drives confidence. The more we love ourselves and produce positive, consistent habits the more our confidence grows. Success grows success. Confidence allows us to perform at the highest level whether it is in the corporate boardroom, the surgery room, on the tennis court, or in the classroom. There is a sweet spot for confidence.

Too much uncontrolled confidence without self-management and you are an arrogant jerk. Too little confidence and you don't show up and speak up for people that need you to have it most. First and foremost, you need to show up and speak up for yourself!

Humility and vulnerability is crucial for healthy confidence and the ability to demonstrate we are all learning, falling down, and getting back up to continue on our journey. A mistake that makes you humble is better than an achievement that makes you arrogant! Focus on small actions that build your confidence because the world begs for more confident people.

Never let success get to your head and never let failure get to your heart. My mantra is **"Don't get too high, don't get too low."** After a successful play, achievement, or victory, we can get too high with emotions leading to arrogance and irrationally thinking we are self-made. After a fumble, failure, or defeat, we can get too low with emotions leading to self-doubt, shutting down, and fear to try again. The sweet spot is in the middle to celebrate wins with humility and gratitude and to rise from losses with resilience and courage. The best athletes do this play-to-play with remarkable composure. This is one distinction of a true pro on and off the field. Think of all the plays throughout your day that can get you too high and too low. Do you get too high after small wins? Do you get too low after small losses? Stay in the middle— even keel—for a big bloom.

Confidence is on a continuum and is situational depending on what is required. The best source of confidence is having self-awareness for where on the continuum one falls for required tasks, roles, and responsibilities. An accurate self-assessment of one's confidence levels for the dynamic gamut of skills and responsibilities is necessary to be successful. A promotion with added responsibilities can shift a normally confident person into a downward spiral of self-doubt. A new software program—or process—which brings a new learning curve can shrink confidence. Likewise, an emotional interaction or event can shift confidence. Be comforted to know that confidence ebbs and flows on the journey for everybody. Sharing lack of confidence in certain areas honestly and openly is actually a huge sign of confidence!

The misconception is that we have to excel at everything and be bulletproof. There couldn't be anything further from the truth. This will lead to exhaustion and disappointment. The great leaders do not feel they need to have confidence in everything they do and surround themselves accordingly with people who have the skills and confidence in their blind spots. Fundamentally, they work smarter, not harder, by not becoming trapped in the tiresome cycle of hiding and artificially bolstering weaknesses. This self-awareness leads to true confidence, improved teamwork, and better engagement.

Think of the best sports teams and their reliance on different talent to win. My best friend in college was the quarterback and I was the wide receiver. I would tell him at practice, "I can't throw but I sure can catch" and he would smile and say back, "I can't catch but I sure can throw." We were a damn good team that won a national championship. Excellence was achieved because we came together from different backgrounds as brothers—a family—with a common vision of winning a championship. Man, I miss playing competitive sports.

It is almost impossible to have real confidence without a commitment to self-awareness. Confidence changes throughout our journey with added responsibilities and the most confident people admit they don't have it all figured out. They surround themselves with an amazing team and wisely seek coaching and mentoring.

What we believe is crucial for our success. I want to share with you two separate stories on the power of mindset. One involving a classmate of mine in high school and the other involving a baseball player.

When I was in high school, one of my classmates, Marvin, was a class clown. Marvin never paid attention in class and had little enthusiasm for learning. He never studied and was about to get kicked out of high school for poor grades.

We all took the SAT in high school, including Marvin. Shockingly, Marvin received notice that he scored a 1440 out of 1600 possible points. This score was not only one of the best in our school's history, but also the state. Teachers and parents became immediately suspicious.

Because of Marvin's history of poor performance, he was investigated for cheating. Marvin firmly assured all, firstly his skeptical mom, he did not cheat. "I took the test, tried my best, and did not cheat," Marvin told everyone. Given the testing room layout and procedures followed, the investigation found the cheating allegation was unsupported. Marvin did not cheat.

After receiving this amazing test score, Marvin then believed he is super smart and started focusing on his education. A complete 180-degree turn in mindset. Limitless thinking. His academic performance improved significantly. Teachers poured their energy into Marvin and encouraged him to attend college. Marvin went to college and continued to excel, becoming a huge success story.

After graduating college, Marvin became a highly successful entrepreneur and businessman. About 15 years later, he received a certified letter in the mail from the SAT Board of Directors that there was a mix-up and that he received the wrong test score way back in high school. His actual score was a subpar 690. Marvin realized in the moment holding the letter that people thought the 1440 changed his life, but the reality was believing and acting like a 1440 is what changed his life. Self-confidence, not aptitude alone, paves your path.

Another story on confidence is more close to our university. We have a damn good baseball program here. Coach reached out to me years ago to work with a pitcher who was struggling with confidence. It is a lot of pressure being a young man standing alone on a mound in front of thousands of fans—a few rudely showing up on social media as cowards.

The player's confidence was completely lost. He was a good pitcher but was stuck. I knew he had great potential and I liked his positive attitude to learn and grow. Talking with him, I knew he was hungry to get his confidence back. I went all in coaching him during the off-season and we were in it together. I was bicycling one afternoon in the city when I came to a stoplight. Watching the stoplight change colors, I had a breakthrough on how I was going to get him back to optimal performance.

I designed a mental skills program for him to rebuild his confidence on the mound. I created **Three Mental Zones: Red, Yellow, and Green.** He had to study the zones. He had to self-monitor throughout his day which color zone he was in. With intense focus, we did guided breathing, visualization, positive affirmations, and emotional agility exercises to transition him from red, to yellow, and ultimately to the green zone. Being human, we found that although the green zone was ideal, it was not realistic for every pitch—every performance. The yellow neutral zone proved to be an effective zone for strong performance. Shifting out of the red zone and not worrying about always being in the green zone was key.

Red Zone: Tired, Anxious, Fearful LOW Confidence

Yellow Zone: Neutral Zone

Green Zone: Calm, Relaxed, Focused HIGH Confidence

The mental skills program I designed was highly successful. This player bounced back and was honored pitcher of the year, along with being named an Academic All-American. He was drafted and played nine seasons in the major leagues, and played in two All-Star games. He now is the chief human resources officer for a Fortune 500 company and is a well-respected servant leader. With admiration, I enjoyed watching his transition into a corporate athlete. We still talk today. The best thing about this guy is you'd never know how much success he has had by the way he treats people. True humility.

Reflection: What daily actions and mindset build your confidence? Who can you surround yourself with that has the skills, thinking, and confidence in your blind spots to complement your strengths? What gets you too high? Too low?

Chapter 18
Self-Compassion

"Good morning Tracy," said Brooks. "Your word is SELF-COMPASSION. Please record what you wish. But before I forget, I want to give you a gift." Brooks handed over a cloth bag and continued to speak in a warm, melodic tone.

Self-compassion will be one of the biggest variables for your quality of life and your journey. How do you love yourself? How do you forgive yourself? What do you believe you deserve? With self-compassion, you will be able to give the world your best. The journey to becoming the best version of ourselves requires us to look back on how far we've come once in a while. We often blame, hurt, and shortchange ourselves because we lack self-compassion and this derails our confidence. Self-compassion is a more effective motivator than self-criticism because its driving power is love. Thriving relationships have individuals who have self-compassion. Colleagues and students who are blooming all have abundant self-compassion. They love themselves a lot and know they deserve love. They do not seek or need external validation to love themselves fully. If your compassion does not include yourself, it is deficient.

Don't let mistakes and failures dry up your self-compassion. We occasionally will display behaviors that are not in alignment with our core values. This is normal because we are human. Humans can be way too critical of themselves. To error is human. We all make mistakes and fail. Be gentle and kind with your self-talk. Monitor your thoughts with discipline. Express self-compassion and forgive yourself daily. It doesn't matter what other people think but it matters a lot what you think about yourself. Like instructed on the airplane before takeoff, put the mask on yourself first. Put yourself first. You deserve the best in life. Practice self-care without guilt. Take a relaxing nap! Life's a marathon, pace yourself. Make loving yourself a priority so you can best love and serve others.

Early in my career, I felt I had to prove myself with excessive work. I pushed and pushed to show my employer and colleagues that I was the real deal. Workaholic. However, this only led to exhaustion and poor performance. I started to practice self-compassion and putting myself first. I said "No" and "Not now" and felt an instant release of stress. At first, there was a transition period of feeling guilty of doing this because I lacked self-compassion to know that this is what I deserved. It felt awkward. However, my deliberate practice of self-care allowed me to show up in the world to serve others. Everything improved.

Employers that put people first are smart because they create healthy cultures of low burnout and high performance and this attracts and retains top talent. You win with good people—and by promoting self-care and family time. **Remember to slow down to speed up and allow others to do the same.** The majority of emails can wait. There is nothing more rewarding in leadership than successfully getting people to slow down and see their self-worth.

As an adult, my dad became one of my best friends. When he was dying in the hospital, he gave me a special gift that was a timeless lesson. As I was visiting with him in his hospital room one morning, he asked me to go into the attic at his house and gave me directions to open a small wooden box. He said that inside the box there would be a watch that my grandfather gave him that he wanted to pass down to me as a family heirloom. The watch was more than 100 years old. My dad shared some stipulations that came with the gift.

"Before I give it to you, go downtown to the local jewelry store, show them this watch, see what they offer, and come back and let me know," my dad instructed. I did this and let him know that I was offered $80 because the jewelry store owner said it was very old.

Next, my dad instructed me to go the pawn shop and do the same. I did this and let him know that I was offered only $20 because the pawn shop owner said it was very worn.

Lastly, my dad instructed me to go to the museum and do the same. I did this and was astonished. The museum curator offered $5,000 for this very rare watch to be included in its precious antiques collection. I told my dad the great news of this marvelous offering price.

My dad taught me the transformational lesson that the right place values you in the right way. He taught me that this goes for the people I surround myself with and places I work. He taught me that if I find myself in the wrong place feeling undervalued not to connect that to my self-worth. "My son, those that know your value will appreciate you," he said. "Every human has amazing value. It is up to people to truly see it in themselves and others."

?

Reflection: What false narratives or experiences are blocking your self-compassion and self-worth? How can you slow down to speed up? When are you most critical of yourself? Is it a fair assessment?

Chapter 19
Life is Better at the Lake

The coffee meetings were giving Brooks energy and inspiration. He never predicted how much better he would feel and the satisfaction he would receive from these meetings with students. Brooks was committed to keeping his terminal illness a secret and wanted to get away for the weekend.

With only a few months to live and a new spike of energy from the coffee meetings, Brooks packed a suitcase for a weekend at one of his favorite lake house rentals to write, kayak, and just be. This, he knew, would be one of his last hurrahs and he was determined to continue to live life to the fullest the best he could. Feeling sorry for himself was never an option.

Being at the lake brought Brooks peace. Many of the best memories of his wife and children were at the lake. In recent years, the lake brought space for restful, reflective solitude. Brooks welcomed solitude but not loneliness—the two were different. He was rarely lonely in his own company which allowed him to fully enjoy life—solo adventures were gratifying. However, loneliness existed with long gaps from friends, family, and his students—missing vital human connection. Brooks became the most lonely when thinking about his wife, his peach, in heaven and his two grown children far away. After his wife's death, Brooks referred to his wife as "my peach in heaven" more times than not when acquaintances curiously asked about her whereabouts, not knowing the tragic story.

Along the way to the lake, Brooks stopped at his favorite cheese store. Out of all the foods on Earth, cheese was at the top of the list. "Cheese enhances clarity," Brooks would tell people with a smile and a chuckle. Brooks arrived to the lake house in the early evening. He unpacked in a bedroom with a sign that read *HEAVEN IS A LITTLE CLOSER IN A HOME BY THE WATER*. The bedroom was on the second-level of the lake house with giant windows showcasing a panoramic view of the lake. Attached to the bedroom was a walkout deck. Brooks stepped out onto it to take in the majestic view—a beautiful rainbow stretched upward into the sky.

The lake water was bright blue towards the middle of the lake. A small wake was churning up soil and sand close to the shore. The water color along the shoreline was muddy brown. As Brooks looked out from the shoreline to the center of the lake, he could tell the water became more brilliantly blue the further from shore. "The majority of people don't have the courage to leave shore, their comfort zone," Brooks wrote in his personal notepad. "Everybody is trampling each other on an overcrowded shore. Real opportunities and less competition is directly proportionate to how far away from shore one is willing to go." Brooks stepped back inside the house, put on his flip flops, and walked down to the shoreline.

He sat in a chair and watched the sunset over and through the trees on the opposite side of the lake. The moment was still and filled with warmth from the last rays of the day's sun. Brooks walked over to a sandy area and picked up a large pebble and tossed it into the water creating a beautiful ripple. The ripple extended infinitely from the original penetration of the water's surface. "We never really know how much we influence the lives of others," Brooks thought to himself as he watched the ripple continue. "When you create a difference in someone's life you not only impact their life, you impact everyone influenced by them in their entire lifetime. It is endless."

Brooks had a wonderful, relaxing weekend at the lake but was looking forward to getting back to his students for the remaining coffee meetings.

Chapter 20
Forgiveness

"Good morning Adriana," said Brooks. "Your word is FORGIVENESS. Please record what you wish. But before I forget, I want to give you a gift." Brooks handed over a cloth bag and continued to speak in a warm, melodic tone.

Forgiveness is the gateway to living in the present moment. Forgiving ourselves for our mistakes big and small and doing the same for others liberates us to truly live here and now. When you forgive, you heal. And when you let go, you grow. The majority of mistakes are completely unintentional. Sadly, some live their whole lives not forgiving people who did them wrong and it doesn't let them fully bloom.

Negative emotions are crucial for the healing process. Disappointment and anger is healthy to express openly and honestly. When you don't let people know that they hurt or disappointed you, you rob them of the opportunity to apologize and make it right. This is emotionally immature. Anyone can respect a person who can put their ego aside and say, "I made a mistake, I apologize, and I am correcting the behavior."

I'd like to share with you my story of forgiveness. When I was about your age, I was boating with good friends on a hot summer day. One of the friends would become my future wife! We had beer, music, and not a worry in the world. I was the designated driver on this particular day and did not drink. The day was perfect so we continued to have fun on the water.

We anchored and were jumping off the boat. The water was like bathwater. Once the sun started to set, we headed back to shore to dock the boat. My best friend, James, wanted to be taken home while everyone else stayed to build a beach bonfire. James and I jumped into my car so I could drive him home and then I planned to return to the bonfire.

By this time, it was dark. We were feeling great from a fun day on the water and the music was loud. We were singing at the top of our lungs, windows down, to Tom Petty – Free Fallin'. James was singing to every word smiling ear-to-ear. I was driving faster than I should have been and lost control on a turn.

We hit a tree and everything went black. I woke up in the hospital. My parents were sitting in the room by my side along with a doctor. The doctor explained that I had already successfully undergone two surgeries and I was going to make a full recovery. I was very lucky.

After one week of being in the hospital, I was able to return home. Once back home, mom and dad came into my bedroom and said they had something they had to tell me. "James suffered even more serious injuries from the accident than you," said my dad with a tear running down his face. "He is alive and recovering, but will not be able to walk normally again."

I had changed my best friend's life forever. I was the driver. The next month after my parents gave me the news about James, I met forgiveness.

While eating breakfast, our doorbell suddenly rang. My mom went to the door and opened it. James hobbled inside on crutches and sat down in our living room. My dad called me into the living room. I was extremely scared. I felt immense guilt.

I started balling hysterically. "Sorry, sorry, so sorry," I cried. James and my parents came over to me and surrounded me with a loving embrace. We cried together as the hurt was shared during the moment. Time stood still. Our shirts became wet with tears. No one was letting go.

As we sat together in the living room, I will never, ever forget the graceful sound of what James said next. "I forgive you Brooks. It was an accident." This was love and forgiveness that I had never felt before in my heart and soul. Receiving this forgiveness gave me the ability to compassionately forgive others throughout my life.

The reality is the people closest to us will hurt and disappoint us the most. The people closest to us will create the biggest wounds. We will also hurt the people closest to us... forgive, heal, and move forward. Bitterness and hate erodes the container that carries it. Life is too short not to forgive ourselves and others with compassion. To error is human, to forgive is divine.

Reflection: Who has hurt you the most? What steps can you take to forgive them and free yourself? Have you fully forgiven yourself for painful mistakes, choices, and accidents on your journey?

Chapter 21
Friendship

"Good morning Chris," said Brooks. "Your word is FRIENDSHIP. Please record what you wish. But before I forget, I want to give you a gift." Brooks handed over a cloth bag and continued to speak in a warm, melodic tone.

Friendship is special. Fellowship warms our hearts and souls. Friendships change over time from acquaintances to deep, trusting friendships and vice versa. You will meet acquaintances with servant hearts that will give you good counsel and opportunities without any expectation in return. Servant leadership is doing positive acts for others without intent to receive anything beneficial in return. However, karma is powerful. This style of leadership rewards abundantly. Pay it forward.

Mentoring is a type of professional friendship that nourishes a big bloom. Mentors will always make time for you and are trusted sounding boards on your journey to becoming the best version of yourself. Strengths, weaknesses, and blind spots are uncovered in our being. Mentors are the compassionate, trusted critics that you go to for advice in challenging situations. With candor, mentors point out possible weeds hindering your bloom. Every plant has their own unique requirements to grow—and so do people. Driven by servant hearts, mentors want to see you succeed personally and professionally. Mentors accelerate growth in identity, dreams, and self-worth. The great mentors will challenge you to go outside your comfort zone.

Great leaders and rising stars have great mentors and a personal board of directors. Growth mindsets, fueled by a strong motivation to improve, attract the best mentors. Personality fit and goals are important for mentor-protégé formation. Individuals who receive mentoring have greater career success, job satisfaction, and leadership potential. Employers of choice have coaching and mentoring in their organizational DNA. Team members are mentored and encouraged to mentor in the community. These organizations put just as much emphasis on personal growth and service to others as professional growth. They employ humanity.

I can tell a lot about friendship considering two factors: time and communication. The healthy, trusting friendships do not need constant communication. Life gets busy. The friendships that last over time are the ones where you do not talk for weeks, months, or even years— but when you do connect you pick up right where you left off from the last time with loving presence. Responding with gratitude to incoming birthday wishes, life milestones, and warm hellos is necessary for friendship to bloom.

Some people confuse friendship as sitting around together staring at phones. This is not real friendship. True friendship is human-to-human over a cup of coffee, helping on a project, and driving the coast together in a convertible. Gaps not talking does not define friendship but giving someone your undivided attention and being there when needed does.

Great friends are hard to come by and people come into our lives to teach us lessons in the moment. These lessons are seeds being planted. Choose friends wisely. Don't worry too much about the number of friends you have at any given moment.

Quality is more important. Four quarters is better than 100 pennies! Spend more time with people who bring out the best in you. Friends believe in you. True friends clap the loudest when you succeed. Surround yourself with the inspired, the motivated, the open-minded, the passionate, and the grateful.

Some of the greatest companions in our lives can have four legs and fur and become as much a part of our family as humans do. Pets teach us important qualities of friendship—unconditional love and the emotional benefits of play. Friendship is fuel to good health and longevity.

Reflection: What friend(s) have made you a better human? How so? How has your friendships changed over time? Who has been your greatest mentor? Who can you count on no matter what?

Chapter 22
Humor

"Good morning Brad," said Brooks. "Your word is HUMOR. Please record what you wish. But before I forget, I want to give you a gift." Brooks handed over a cloth bag and continued to speak in a warm, melodic tone.

Humor is the antidote to the messiness of life. Humans are unpredictable and do pretty interesting things. Humor helps us appreciate the unpredictable and surprising behaviors in good spirits. Humor goes a long way in storytelling awkward experiences in our shared humanity. It helps us lift people up, and not take life too seriously or feel alone during challenges. For a happier life, stop taking everything so seriously. Life does not have to be perfect to be wonderful. Be sure to laugh at the mess and confusion every once in a while.

The best workplaces have fun. They smile and laugh. Humor has an abundance of benefits including strengthening the immune system and reducing stress and anxiety. All humans smile and laugh in the same language! Childlike wonder is not serious but is filled with curiosity, play, and laughter. Six-year-olds laugh an average of 300 times a day. Adults? Adults on average laugh less than 50 times a day. A big bloom never outgrows humor. I want to share with you one of my favorite jokes.

A guy was stuck on his rooftop in a flood. He was scared and praying to God for help.

Soon a woman in a rowboat came by and shouted to the guy on the roof, "Jump in, I can save you."

The stranded man shouted back, "No, it's OK, I'm praying to God and he is going to save me."

So the rowboat continued on.

Then a speedboat came by. "The man in the speedboat shouted, "Jump in, I can save you."

To this the stranded man said, "No thanks, I'm praying to God and he is going to save me. I have faith."

So the speedboat continued on.

Then a helicopter came by and the pilot shouted down, "Grab this rope and I will lift you to safety."

To this the stranded man again replied, "No thanks, I'm praying to God and he is going to save me. I have faith."

So the helicopter reluctantly flew away.

Soon the water rose above the rooftop and the man drowned. He went to Heaven. He finally got his chance to discuss this whole situation with God, at which point he exclaimed, "I had faith in you but you didn't save me, you let me drown. I don't understand why!"

To this God replied, "I sent you a rowboat, a speedboat, and a helicopter, what more did you want?"

Reflection: How can you lighten up? What are you too serious about in life? What is your favorite joke you can share with others to inspire laughter?

Chapter 23
Gratitude

"Good morning Russell," said Brooks. "Your word is GRATITUDE. Please record what you wish. But before I forget, I want to give you a gift." Brooks handed over a cloth bag and continued to speak in a warm, melodic tone.

Gratitude is awareness of all the blessings surrounding us. Blessings are people, experiences, opportunities, and things that add value, convenience, beauty, or comfort to our lives. When we deliberately appreciate blessings in the present moment, we express gratitude. Gratitude is the human emotion that erases entitlement. There is someone out there dreaming and praying for the life you are living right now. The happiest people have gratitude and are not chasing materialistic, superficial things to fill a void. Gratitude turns what we have in the present moment into enough. Strong negative emotions and challenging circumstances can be successfully tamed by responding with gratitude.

The benefits of gratitude are endless. Gratitude improves sleep quality, lowers blood pressure, increases energy, reduces stress, and helps you live longer. Writing down what you are grateful for and why when you wake up in the morning and before you go to bed are the perfect bookends to a sometimes messy day. The universe rewards a gratitude mindset. Have you thought of keeping a gratitude journal? This will nourish your bloom.

Joy and happiness is found in moments of gratitude. Comparing our lives to others suppresses gratitude. The more thankful we are for everything we have, the more happiness we may experience. What if you woke up this morning with only what you thanked God for yesterday?

When my kids were teenagers, they had little appreciation for all that they had. They had a nice home with fresh food and clean water. They had a safe community with nice parks and a state-of-the-art swimming pool. A great school. They had nice clothes and new shoes every year. But with all these blessings, they lacked gratitude. They compared themselves to others focusing on all that they didn't have instead of appreciating all that they did have, creating unhappiness. This brought me frustration. We took a "vacation" that they would never forget. This was no trip to Disney World.

We visited an impoverished city in Latin America. The water was unclean. Roads were dirt. Street beggars were on every corner. There was no convenience of fast-food restaurants. Citizens had barely enough to survive. My kids' eyes were wide-open. With a group from our church, we built a building from nothing. This small building was erected to be used as a health care clinic. Day-by-day we built the clinic until it was completed within one month. We also helped local community leaders create a facility to generate clean water. Out of all the natural resources to be thankful for, I am most thankful for clean drinking water. We must always vigilantly protect our freshwater resources.

Our group felt immense gratitude on this trip. My kids returned home with a newly found gratitude and eagerness to serve others. There was little complaining after this experience!

Gratitude is accessible at all times in both trial and triumph. It is not only inward. Showing gratitude outwardly towards others is leadership. Giving out kudos is gratitude. People who feel appreciated will always do more than what is expected. It costs nothing to say a simple "Thank You," "I appreciate you," and "We'd be lost without you." Servant leaders demonstrate gratitude. You inspire others by showing them how amazing they are with affectionate gratitude.

Reflection: What are you most grateful for? Where in your day can you create mini-moments for gratitude? Is your gratitude more intense during trial or triumph? Who has done something you appreciated? Have you taken time to thank them?

Chapter 24
Tree of Better Versions

It was a comfortable, early Saturday morning so Brooks decided to go for a bike ride. The route of choice this day was one that was heading away from the city. Looking down at his watch, Brooks decided he would turn back around once he hit eight miles.

At about seven miles, there was a path that he had never seen before on this route that bended into the woods. The path was marked and paved for cyclists so Brooks took it feeling explorative. The path took him along a river and further back into the woods where it became darker and cooler from the shade of the trees.

Large trees were everywhere with thick branches. Brooks was intrigued by how far away from city life he felt with his present surroundings. He took a seat on a bench that had a memoriam on it with a couples name reading *GOODNIGHT SWEETHEART, I'LL SEE YOU IN THE MORNING.*

As Brooks sat sweaty on the bench, he couldn't help but notice one massive tree. An arborist professor once told him that a tree's roots can be a mirror reflection in the ground as the tree size above the ground. Brooks imagined how expansive the roots must go into the soil with this mesmerizing tree.

"Roots. They ground us and give us guidance as our core

values," he wrote in his personal notepad perspiration mostly dried now. "There are too many people and organizations that don't have roots. They are indifferent in a world that begs for conviction."

With his abundant experience advising organizations, Brooks found that the organizations that had strong core values were always ahead of the competition—especially during adversity. Core values made decision-making easier aligning to the roots of the organization. Values like integrity, service to others, always giving your best, compassion, and authenticity. The individuals and organizations that truly achieve excellence understand with clarity their roots, values, and their story.

Brooks recalled the nostalgia he felt when returning to his hometown, his roots. He would walk past his former home, elementary school, church, and friends' homes with intense memories and emotions of gratitude. There were so many people from his childhood that positively shaped who he had become that he didn't fully appreciate until many years later. All the teachers, neighbors, friends, parents, organizations, and random community acts of kindness. Many of these people now had relocated or were no longer alive. "Everybody should go back to their hometown every now and then to remember who they were and reflect on how far they have come," Brooks thought focusing in on the massive trunk of the tree still imagining the deep roots below the surface. "It's a great reminder of the start to our life story. As adults, we need to be the type of person who we needed as a child."

Still looking at the tree from the bench, Brooks thought of every business as a tree with their roots as core values and history. He thought about his favorite football team the Green Bay Packers and how once every player, coach, and staff member signed with the organization they instantly represented the rich history and legacy of the organization.

They immediately joined greatness and were acutely aware of becoming part of the legacy. This interconnectedness fertilizes passion and excellence. "Leaders must share and inspire the organization's story to connect people to its roots," Brooks would advise his clients. "People need to become excited about something bigger than themselves." At the end of the day, every human needs to feel the satisfaction that they are part of an inspiring story making the world a better place.

Brooks started to gaze way up to the top of the tree where a bird was sitting on a branch at the highest point. The bird flew away as simultaneously another bird landed much lower on the tree near the trunk. "The organizations achieving excellence are like trees in that they are the structure to help people land, grow, and then soar personally and professionally," Brooks reminded himself. These organizations are what Brooks called "trees of better versions" as structures deliberately creating better versions of people—employers of choice.

When organizations prioritize creating better versions of people, everything else naturally falls into place. Putting people first is necessary for excellence. Brooks would even challenge leaders to facilitate and coach some of their best employees once they plateaued or felt stuck to fly away outside the organization. This approach, although at times feeling counterproductive, actually created a robust talent pipeline being an organization rooted in creating better versions of people to grow and soar.

"The way your employees feel when they leave your organization is just as important as when they arrived," Brooks would say at HR conferences. "Ask if you can help them transition into their next chapter, treat them with dignity, and never burn a bridge." With a people-first culture of developing and growing people, there is always top talent flying in to land with these employers of choice.

"We are all born to soar, to bloom" Brooks thought as he hopped off the bench and back onto his bike. "Leaders just facilitate the process."

Chapter 25
Love

"Good morning Chloe," said Brooks. "Your word is LOVE. Please record what you wish. But before I forget, I want to give you a gift." Brooks handed over a cloth bag and continued to speak in a warm, melodic tone.

Love is the source of all good in the world. Where there is a lot of good being done, there is a lot of love. We need to love ourselves first so we can love and serve others. Love spills from the heart and is the catalyst for forgiving ourselves and others. The older you become, the more you will realize it isn't about material things, pride, or ego…it is about our hearts and who they beat for. With each act, create pause to ask yourself "Do my actions come from a place of love?" All we need is love in our homes, workplaces, and communities.

The average human spends more than 90,000 hours at work in their lifetime. Now this is a lot of time! We must love what we do for our profession. The thriving workplaces have people who love what they do. They love serving internally and externally. There is passion in the details and they love the mission and vision of the organization. Similarly, the thriving homes have people who love what they do for work. When one does not love what they do at work, they come home irritable, frustrated, and wilted. This affects relationships with family and friends. Find your passion and have urgency to do what you love. Help others find their passion. Create a list of all the things personally and professionally you love to do. There will be crossover and crystallization. The only way to do great work is to love what you do. You will know when you find it. Do what you love and you will never have a problem with Mondays.

We think we fully comprehend love until we lose something we love that can never be replaced. It is, at that moment, we meet love. I'm not talking about losing your gloves on a winter day. I'm talking about losing the love of your life instantly. My wife, my peach, was taken from us way too soon in a car accident. I had rage and extreme pain. I blamed God. I blamed myself. But, you see, I couldn't escape love. Love poured in from family, friends, and the community to help us heal and move forward. I've seen this same love from our community over and over throughout the years when experiencing crises. It is during the worst times of your life that you will feel the warm colors of the true, loyal blooms all around you.

To fully experience real love, we must allow our hearts to become unguarded and completely vulnerable knowing it is beating out in the open among the pain of the world. As humans, to be the turtle that removes its shell so it can courageously love and feel love even with thorny, painful patches along the journey. Raw, painful, magically beautiful, authentic love.

Bonding during adversity is critical for our emotional health. Each one of us will be called to step up in our lifetime and absolutely pour our love into someone that is hurting. I look back and will never, ever forget the love that flowed into my heart and soul from this university community. My wife still beats in my heart and inspires me every day. Amazing healing happens when relationships, workplaces, and communities are united in endless love.

Reflection: What do you love most about your work, hobbies, and beyond? What is your #1 passion? When on your journey have you felt or given the most love?

Chapter 26
Kindness

"Good morning Alonzo," said Brooks. "Your word is KINDNESS. Please record what you wish. But before I forget, I want to give you a gift." Brooks handed over a cloth bag and continued to speak in a warm, melodic tone.

Kindness fills humans up. Schools, churches, workplaces, neighborhoods, and communities bloom with small acts of kindness. No act of kindness is ever too small and it often makes a greater ripple in the world than we can ever comprehend. Treat people with kindness, even when they disagree with you. Generosity and kindness always make things better.

Practicing self-compassion, accept kindness. A healthy worldview is that the majority of people are intentionally and authentically trying their best to be kind. Kindness is best learned by accepting and feeling it. If you are a natural giver, it may be challenging to receive generosity or ask for help. Giving kindness becomes even more joyful once we learn to receive kindness.

When I was younger, it was easy for me to give but hard for me to receive. It felt awkward to accept compliments, gifts, and help. I would not fully accept compliments with gratitude, and would not even say "Thank You" but rather give a half smile. My inability to fully receive kindness was confusing. I felt sad that I could not share the affection in my heart for people's kindness towards me. With coaching, I realized my self-compassion needed a boost and other people struggled with this just like me. We all deserve to receive kindness! Once self-compassion was well established, I deliberately accepted the incoming kindness—and I was able to push it back out into the world tenfold. This growth has resulted in improved positive human connection. Confident, self-compassionate people embrace compliments—and kindness.

I'd like to share with you a story on kindness. We moved around a lot when I was a small boy because of my dad's sales career. Big cities were our landing spots which had their pros and cons. One big advantage of living in the city was that we had famous musicians and artists come to the city, one being a world-class violinist. When I was 11-years-old, my mom and dad took me to hear her play at the most beautiful auditorium in the city. The music was heavenly. My dad—a man with terrific people skills and a big heart —talked to her backstage after the performance, inviting her to come to our home for food, drink, and fellowship. She accepted and ended up playing a private concert for us and friends in our living room.

I will never forget sitting in our own home in complete awe listening to one of the greatest violinists in the world. A spontaneous event turned into wonderment. She played for us as if she were still back at the auditorium in front of the sellout crowd. Music flowed as she was completely centered in the moment. This was pure mindfulness, passion, and excellence. "If you are going to take the time to listen to me play, I have an obligation to give you my best all the time," I remember her graciously telling us on our front porch before leaving. Kindness came together from my family's warm hospitality and her willingness to accept the invite. I remember that night like it was yesterday and will never forget the kindness and performance. Because of this experience, I have had a lifelong love for the violin and orchestra.

Compassion is kindness in full bloom. I'm not impressed by money, social status, or job title…I'm impressed by the way someone treats other human beings with kindness and makes them feel welcomed. You are never too important to be kind to people. Any day you could be standing next to someone who is trying their best not to wilt and fall apart. You never completely know what people are dealing with in their personal life. Always be kind—it's that simple. Be the type of person that makes everyone you encounter feel perfectly okay with being exactly who they are. Everybody matters. In a world where you can be anything—be kind.

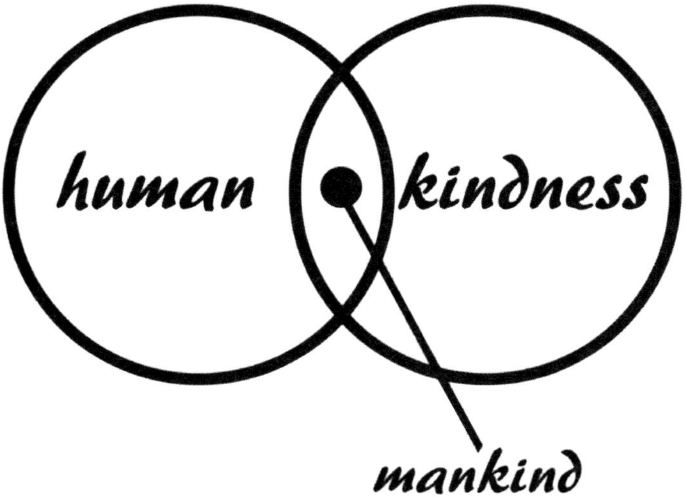

Reflection: What small acts of kindness can you show others? Do you fully receive and embrace kindness?

Chapter 27
Authenticity

"Good morning Maria," said Brooks. "Your word is AUTHENTICITY. Please record what you wish. But before I forget, I want to give you a gift." Brooks handed over a cloth bag and continued to speak in a warm, melodic tone.

Authenticity is being true to yourself and others. When you are living an authentic life, you are living your truth and what you say, think, and do is in harmony. Your head, heart, and core are in balance—full body flow. A lot of time is lost being disingenuous trying to gain others' unnecessary approval. Sadly, I've watched friends live their lives based on their parents' expectations.

Authenticity is giving yourself permission to be vulnerable. No one has life completely figured out—nor do they have all the answers! The best human connection often happens by sharing our weaknesses. There is an obsession about being happy at all times—this is unrealistic! The magic is in the mess. Staying positive doesn't mean you have to avoid negative emotions and be happy all the time. Positivity is the vision on hard days that better days are coming and having discipline to visualize the bloom.

A good day is filled with a mix of positive and negative emotions. Negative emotions make us human, build our resiliency, strengthen our character, and illuminate positive emotions. Negative emotions give us wisdom and have an upside when managed successfully. The most positive exponential growth comes from negative emotions. We all have stress. I always can tell how big of a bloom a student will have by how they manage their stress in and outside the classroom. Healthy stress management can be done with:

- Exercise
- Writing and journaling
- Eating healthy and nutritious foods
- Art and creative hobbies
- Volunteering in the community
- Drinking plenty of water
- Meditation and prayer
- Reading inspiring books
- Being with nature, pets, and positive people

I had shock and denial when my wife suddenly died. I had tremendous anger and sorrow. These emotions, although extremely painful and intense, were the start of the healing process. These painful emotions were healthy and the only way out of the darkness to continue onward. I had to embrace anger and rage in my grieving. It is better to feel pain than nothing at all.

It is exhausting and unrealistic to portray constant happiness. Authentic being is experiencing all emotions. Western culture is particularly obsessed with being happy all the time. I ask my students every year, "Raise your hand if you feel you should—even when you are not—be happy at all times." All hands go straight up. I follow by asking, "How many of you think it would be a huge relief if you didn't have to act happy 24/7?" All hands go straight up and there is a collective exhale. I am not sure why so much time is exhausted on cultivating a 24/7 highlight reel of happiness on social media. Please know and be comforted that this content is occasionally artificial. Truly happy people are too busy enjoying the present moment to be posting about it on social media.

Our workplaces and society need to embrace negative emotions and the wisdom these negative emotions provide. Surprisingly, I have found in coaching that when there is transformational positive growth grief is often present. Why? People have powerfully transformed to the extent that they actually go through a process of grieving the loss of their old self—now that's growth! Emotional agility is being positive and human while experiencing negative emotions. Suppressing and burying intense negative emotions is like shaking up a soda can and putting it back in the fridge. It will have to be released sometime. Manage your emotions. Sit with it. Feel it. Bring it close. Open it.

People would rather follow someone who is always real than one who is always right. Leaders promote authenticity, passionate dialogue, and healthy conflict. Showing your humanity goes a long way in leadership. **The best leaders are not perfect. The best leaders are authentic—and human.**

Authentic feedback is at the core of successful coaching. Candor often activates negative emotions but demonstrates that people care about you and your growth. No coaching can actually be a sign that people have given up on you or don't care, so be sure to embrace feedback. Not providing feedback robs an individual the opportunity to grow—to improve. Avoiding or sugarcoating feedback does not promote growth. If you had a piece of food stuck in your teeth, would you want to be told? Of course! Growth mindsets are always seeking feedback and opportunities to improve. Providing authentic feedback with composure, compassion, and empathy is imperative to be a great coach and leader. Receiving authentic feedback with composure, gratitude, and a willingness to improve is crucial to be a great employee—great teammate. Compassionate, authentic coaching is fertilization for a beautiful bloom.

I was coaching an executive last year who was severely challenged with organizational culture. "We lack having crucial conversations with candor Brooks," she said. "There is toxic passive-aggressiveness, ego, sugarcoating, backstabbing, and drama."

After performing a culture audit, I found that the behaviors and systems in place were extremely inauthentic—with a focus on creating a culture of nonstop happiness rather than communicating hard truths and accountability. This was admirable—but utopian and superficial. I call it the "unicorn culture." It looked good above the surface but below the surface there were big, ugly weeds. This culture stifled authentic, negative emotions that actually made employees feel real and whole. It prevented people from speaking up to honestly challenge people, processes, and ideas. People were silenced and there was bullying. Authenticity was desperately needed below the surface.

We collaborated to design a more authentic culture where everybody could bring their human to work. The company invited and challenged all to let their true selves shine. Real negative emotions were celebrated. Individual strengths, weaknesses, and personality profiles were shared internally. A trusting team emerged from everybody seeing others' strengths as a complement to their weaknesses and not a threat to position or authority.

We made Emotional Intelligence a core value to professionally and civilly communicate negative emotions and feedback with candor. Negative emotions were no longer checked at the door entering the workplace. Employees were trained to have tough, direct conversations performed with self-awareness, adaptability, and empathy. Within six months, the results were remarkable. Creativity, innovation, and morale spiked. Customer service improved. Everybody felt engaged and valued. There was positive growth. Drama and passive-aggressiveness dissolved. Top talent gravitated towards the company. Oh, and there was more happiness.

Reflection: How can you become more positive and composed while experiencing negative emotions? How do you, your workplace, and society view negative emotions? What is a personal or professional success story from a negative emotion(s)? What does authentic leadership mean to you?

Chapter 28
Courage

“Good morning Mark,” said Brooks. “Your word is COURAGE. Please record what you wish. But before I forget, I want to give you a gift.” Brooks handed over a cloth bag and continued to speak in a warm, melodic tone.

Courage is the fire we bring to our dreams and ideas. It gives us the ability to go outside our comfort zone to become the best versions of ourselves for our families, communities, and the world. Great things never come from comfort zones. Doing what is right is not always popular, easy, or applauded. Having integrity and doing what is right takes courage.

In my life, I have found conviction and core values can wilt without great courage. Remaining silent on what sets you passionately on fire and what you believe in is extremely painful. Have you felt the pain of remaining silent when someone was unkind or hurtful? We have all been there when someone says something disrespectful or unkind to us—or someone around us—and we didn’t speak up and call them out. Leadership is speaking up and courageously protecting those in your care. Exceptional leaders have conviction—not sitting on the sidelines indifferent watching and tolerating things that they know are completely out of line. Have the courage to lead.

Embracing imperfection is courageous. We are conditioned at a young age that perfection is success. It takes courage to be vulnerable and perfectly imperfect. Unfortunately, young boys are misguided that showing emotion is weakness while young girls are misguided that showing perfection is strength. This mindset has consequences years later in our relationships, homes, workplaces, and communities. Authenticity and being fully human is perfection!

Leaning into negative emotions is courageous. The biggest growth in life comes from pain and discomfort. It takes tremendous courage to truly feel and sit with pain. The majority of societal problems we face today are the byproduct of humanity not having the courage to go outside individual comfort zones and authentically lean into negative emotions. Instead, we run from or suppress the negative emotions—and avoid crucial conversations. If a conversation is hard, it's probably the one worth having. Great leaders facilitate hard conversations with Emotional Intelligence.

Courage is showing up, speaking up, and genuinely sharing your ideas and convictions. Showing vulnerability is courageous—I have yet to meet someone courageous that has not authentically faced their fear, pain, and wounds. If we want success, we must get comfortable being uncomfortable. Every next chapter of your life will demand a different you. Be brave enough to suck at something new. There will be a day that comes when the risk to remain tight in the bud is more painful than the risk to bloom. Go for it, play big. The big bloom happens outside your comfort zone with great courage.

Reflection: What courageous action can you take to get outside your comfort zone? What does courageous leadership mean to you?

Chapter 29
Discipline

"Good morning Denzel," said Brooks. "Your word is DISCIPLINE. Please record what you wish. But before I forget, I want to give you a gift." Brooks handed over a cloth bag and continued to speak in a warm, melodic tone.

Discipline is small daily choices to achieve dreams and goals. Establishing self-control is greatness simplified. Discipline, with self-awareness and clarity, is the consistent choices to manage instant gratification and emotional impulses. Discipline fertilizes a big bloom. Emotional impulses are weeds to discipline and are all around us. We are bombarded daily with unhealthy options that detour us from our best versions.

Discipline in the moment is where goals, dreams, and relationships are won and lost. Make a commitment to create space, to create pause, in the mini-moments of conversations and choices. An emotional impulse will be weakened within six seconds. Six seconds is a long time when you are emotionally hijacked—temporarily numbing clarity. One tool is to envision the best version of yourself during the six seconds to regain composure and alignment with your goals. A vivid image in your head of your very best self. For example, create a buffer space to visualize your most fit self when making choices of what to eat and portion size. Envisioning wearing your favorite pants—the ones that fit just right—will increase discipline to make better food choices.

Reactionary words and choices rarely have value and are the byproduct of deficient discipline. Having the discipline to create space leads to improved listening and more thoughtful questions, responses, choices, and ultimately—behavior. For example, have you ever drafted an email—refrained from sending it because you were upset—and the next morning were glad you didn't hit send? Great leadership is having composure when others are overreacting. **Before you speak, pause and THINK:**

T– is it TRUE?
H– is it HELPFUL?
I– is it INSPIRING?
N– is it NECESSARY?
K– is it KIND?

It is hard to find a highly successful person that does not have discipline in their life. They are consistent and this pays huge dividends. They have healthy habits driven by discipline. When to awake. What to eat. How much to exercise. What to say yes to. What to say no to. Discipline is a muscle. The more we exercise discipline, the stronger it becomes. Success breeds success. The more discipline you have the easier life becomes.

Reflection: What areas of your life need more discipline to achieve your dreams and goals? How can you intentionally create space to make better choices and responses?

Chapter 30
Resilience

“Good morning Monica,” said Brooks. “Your word is RESILIENCE. Please record what you wish. But before I forget, I want to give you a gift.” Brooks handed over a cloth bag and continued to speak in a warm, melodic tone.

Resilience is learning how to surf when the huge waves of life come rolling towards us. The giant leaps of personal growth come from adversity, setbacks, and failure. Falling teaches us how to get back up and roll with the punches! Negative emotions experienced during adversity plant us for exponential positive growth.

A resilient mindset is one that finds the gifts that emerge from challenges. Gratitude and a growth mindset is the nourishment for resilience, grit, and grace. Just as anxiety and drama can spread like wildfire through the workplace, so can gratitude and generosity. Positive growth does not come from avoiding adversity but rather seeing the gifts, silver linings, and teachings from the setbacks and challenges. A mantra I have used with success to become more resilient is the simple saying, “We’ll See.” It is a declaration of faith and letting go of control. The positive affirmation **“We’ll See”** almost instantly brings calm and peace.

Envisioning a positive, future bloom is essential for emotional resiliency. We all experience challenges, valleys, and darkness on our journey. During this adversity, one must be able to have a vision for something budding in the future to avoid becoming emotionally paralyzed, stuck, and hopeless. Looking backward with negative thoughts fertilizes the weeds…be careful! Positive growth happens when you have something to look forward to in the future. This event could be anything from envisioning a relaxing vacation, to passing the exam, to seeing the best version of yourself. Anticipating a future bloom provides emotional resiliency to successfully manage adversity, boredom, and challenging situations.

When you're in a dark place you might think you've been buried but actually you have been planted for a beautiful bloom! Embrace the suck. Don't hide or turn to negative habits to cope. Resilience is endurance to go on even when nothing changes. The greater your capacity for endurance and discipline, the more rewards that will come your way. The amazing rewards never come instantaneously.

There are silver linings from setbacks. Practice self-awareness to notice these nutrients planted. Ask "What is this teaching me?" and "How can I face this wave head on and surf with it?" Being able to manage adversity and negative emotions is important to who we will become. No one is entitled to be happy all the time and have everything always go in their favor. Every setback begs for a giant comeback. It is during the struggles, the pain, and the setbacks when our character blooms.

Reflection: What are the major setbacks in your life that strengthened your character? What current setback in your life begs for a giant comeback? What emotion makes you tougher and stronger?

Chapter 31
Last Attempts to Connect

A final wish of Brooks was to connect with his children by phone to let them know of his illness and the reality of his looming death. They lived thousands of miles away and had avoided him for years. His children had deep wounds from years ago that were never healed. The epicenter of these wounds were their mother's tragic car accident. Brooks was beloved by his students, colleagues, and community but not his own children. This was painful and confusing.

Although he had two biological children, Brooks viewed all his students as children of his own, too. With love, he cared deeply for their growth. He felt a responsibility to care for his students as if they were his own children. The university had students from all over the world and this gave Brooks even more intention to love and serve his students. He would scan his class every year and think to himself, "Wow, these are all someone's precious child in my care." With many of his students graduating and moving on to their next chapters entering the workforce, Brooks challenged leaders in the business community to think about this leadership philosophy and to continue to take good care of them, too.

Brooks was optimistic. Maybe he would successfully reach his distant biological children at this attempt in his life. If any, this was the time to connect. He dialed at several different times of day with no success always hanging up before the beep to leave a message. He decided that he would try one more time and if there was no answer he would leave a brief message.

He dialed and received the familiar voicemail. He left a message. “Hello,” said Brooks with a scratch in his voice. “I wanted to give you a call and let you know that I think about you a lot. You will always be my sunshine. I have not been feeling well but my doctors are great. If I don’t hear back from you, it would bring me much joy if you would visit the university at May graduation. Always know…I love you.”

Brooks hung up the phone and cried uncontrollably. It felt good to cry this hard.

Chapter 32
Faith

Lou was the final student to meet with Professor Brooks Lambeau at the assigned times at the university coffeehouse. By this point in the semester, Brooks had spent enough time at the coffeehouse that the staff looked forward to serving him and hearing his friendly wit. Like his students, Brooks knew every staff member by name and what they were most passionate about in life. The staff would have his favorite medium roast coffee and bagel in the works as soon as they saw him enter the cafe.

"Good morning Lou," said Brooks. "Your word is FAITH. Please record what you wish. But before I forget, I want to give you a gift." Brooks handed over a cloth bag and continued to speak in a warm, melodic tone.

Faith is to believe. Faith is to believe not by sight but by how we are inwardly transformed in mind, heart, and soul by the belief. Where there is love, kindness, forgiveness, and grace—there is God. God is the source to a beautiful, eternal bloom. Connect to the source with prayer.

Prayer is an immediate boost to our health. Spiritual meditation significantly improves mental and emotional health outcomes as well as suppressing the fight or flight response, making one less hyper-reactive to negative emotions. Both negative and positive emotions should be explored in prayer as well as what can and cannot be controlled. Great leaders continuously discern what they can and cannot control. Discernment boosts clarity and leads to a warm confidence. A simple yet powerful spiritual meditation is the **Serenity Prayer:**

"God, grant me the serenity to accept
the things I cannot change,
The courage to change the things I can,
And the wisdom to know the difference."

Faith is having a relationship with God that gives us the courage, confidence, and grace here on Earth. **Faith allows us to live boldly.** Be who God calls you to be. Accept the light—then be the light. God has plans to prosper you. Be courageous enough to listen beyond the worldly noise! Faith is a journey with many tests, peaks, and valleys. Don't use your energy to worry, use your energy to believe and trust. Faith and fear cannot occupy us at the same time.

Just like carrying a heavy backpack hour after hour can become tiresome, carrying fear and worries is extremely heavy too. Prayer allows the release of the weight. It's extremely exhausting trying to control everything. When I've had suffering and confusion on my journey, I've heard angels whisper in my ear "Let Go, Let God." Letting go is emotional maturity—spiritual maturity. Connecting with the Holy Spirit, we are all growing and blooming together. At the end of the day, we are all walking each other home.

Reflection: What things do you need to let go of and give to God's care? How can you best share your God-given gifts, love, kindness, and light with the world?

Chapter 33
Transitions

It quickly became mid-October as Brooks had finished his last scheduled coffee meeting. Autumn leaves were turning burnt orange and fire red on campus which Brooks always enjoyed. Seasonal change was a natural reminder of the ongoing transitions in life. "The reality is we are all in transition," Brooks thought as he walked the campus inhaling the fresh, crisp air. "Transitioning from endings so we can connect with new beginnings."

Chapter 34
Final Assignment

Professor Brooks Lambeau's "Emotional Intelligence for 21st Century Leadership" class was now together in late October. Brooks, standing in front of the entire class, gave his final goodbye.

"I hope your semester is going well," Brooks said to his class. "I am happy to report not one of you missed your assigned coffee meeting with me. Thank you for your time and presence."

Students were engaged and listening. Unlike some other professors, Brooks had the respect of his students by the way he led his life. Brooks continued speaking to his class in a more quiet voice and revealed his terminal illness.

"I am dying and will not be around to see you graduate in May. This will be our last class together. Your final assignment and my last request is that you come together this week outside the student union where graduation will be held in spring—and that you plant all the tulip bulbs I gifted each one of you inside the cloth bags at our meetings. The university maintenance and grounds team has already prepared the soil at this location for you. In a different way, I have prepared it for you too. Next, I want you to convene as a group and discuss what you learned from our coffee meetings and write down a summary. If you feel inspired, please share your summary at May graduation.

It's time for me to reunite with my peach. I wish you all an endless bloom."

The classroom was absolutely silent. Professor Brooks Lambeau walked out of his classroom for the last time and passed on five weeks later.

Chapter 35
Graduation Day

It was a beautiful May graduation day. The university terrace was filled with administration, professors, alumni, community, and students. The band played and the outdoor air was filled with celebration and excitement of endless possibilities. Professor Brooks Lambeau's children, mourning their father and remembering his last request, were in attendance. The death of their father had made them realize how much time they had foolishly lost with an amazing human being and how much they loved and admired him.

William, a student of Professor Lambeau's class, was selected by his peers as the speaker for the graduation ceremony.

"Thank you all for coming to this special day," said William. "My fellow students and I learned a lot over the years here but not one of us learned more than when we met with the late Professor Brooks Lambeau. He taught us about faith, courage, love, and kindness. He taught us about resilience, gratitude, time, and forgiveness. To honor him and to celebrate his life, we collectively wanted to share with you what we learned from Professor Brooks Lambeau."

With the tulips in full bloom covering the university grounds for all to see, William took out a piece of paper titled "Endless Bloom" and continued to speak in a warm, melodic tone.

Chapter 36
Endless Bloom

Life is an endless bloom,
One human growing the next,

Nourishing each other to bloom,
A journey of dreams, resilience, and courage,

Life is an endless bloom,
Planting love, forgiveness, and faith,

Living a big bloom,
A colorful, real bloom,

Life is an endless bloom,
Covering the gardens of our hearts,

Connecting with the Holy Spirit,
Opening us fully for an eternal bloom,

Life is an endless bloom,
Walking each other home.

Employ Humanity Leadership Training

employ humanity®
Inspiring Emotional Intelligence in humans and the workplace

Bill Marklein founded Employ Humanity LLC to inspire Emotional Intelligence in workplaces across the world. Emotional Intelligence is the ability to successfully manage our own emotions and the emotions around us and it is the #1 competency for servant leadership, building trusting relationships, and inspiring humanity in the 21st Century. Emotional Intelligence is not a luxury, it's a necessity for excellence in business and life and is the foundation for optimizing human potential.

Contact Employ Humanity to book inspiring keynotes, seminars, on-site training, off-site retreats, virtual learning, and to order this book and other resources for your team(s).

Website: employhumanity.com

Email: sayhello@employhumanity.com